DONE.

DONE.

A COOK'S GUIDE TO

knowing when

 FOOD IS

Perfectly Cooked

JAMES PETERSON

CHRONICLE BOOKS

SAN FRANCISCO

Library of Congress Cataloging-in-Publication Data:

Peterson, James.
Done : a cook's guide to knowing when food is
perfectly cooked / James Peterson.
    pages cm
Includes index.
ISBN 978-1-4521-1963-2 (alkaline paper)
1. Cooking. I. Title.
TX652.P46 2014
641.3–dc23
2013026809

Manufactured in China

Designed by William van Roden
Cover design by Vanessa Dina and William van Roden

10 9 8 7 6 5 4 3 2 1

Chronicle Books LLC
680 Second Street
San Francisco, California 94107
www.chroniclebooks.com

Acknowledgments

While seemingly a simple book about a simple subject, the production of a book like this takes a mammoth amount of energy from a surprising number of people.

My first thanks are to Lorena Jones, my editor, for her enthusiasm, conscientiousness, and eye for detail. She has taken care of me throughout the yearlong process of writing the initial manuscript. Her criticisms are thoughtful but never barbed.

And while I hate to admit her job is as difficult as it is, I must thank copy editor Jane Tunks for her incredible thoroughness. Working with her has been a real pleasure and has taught me how to be a better writer.

The book's sprightly design came as a complete surprise, as I never would have envisioned something so dynamic and full of color. Thanks must go to Vanessa Dina and William van Roden.

Shooting the pictures was the hardest part of producing this book. I must thank Nate Meshberg for his unstinting effort, assistance, and creative input in producing the photography. Working with him was such a pleasure.

And then there are those in my personal life who keep me going and on the straight and narrow. My agents Elise and Arnold Goodman are always there for me and guide me through projects large and small. My appreciation is limitless. I also thank Joel Hoffman for his guidance and professionalism. And I must never forget my friends, without whom little would seem possible.

Last and of course not least, I must thank my husband, Zelik Mintz, for simply being there.

DONE. CONTENTS

Introduction

When people asked me what I was working on as I was writing this book and I told them a book about doneness, there was a moment's hesitation, as though they didn't hear me quite right. It was only when I explained how determining doneness is the Achilles' heel of many a would-be confident cook that their faces brightened up with understanding.

Cooking is the application of heat to various foods using a limited number of methods and for varying periods of time. Most cooking techniques are straightforward. You put something in the oven to roast it, or in a frying pan to sauté it, or you put it on the grill. The trick is to know when to stop cooking.

Many of us don't even recognize properly cooked foods, much less how to prepare them. A well-roasted chicken is still pink inside the thigh, and a grilled scallop should be translucent. Pork or veal chops should be cooked medium, not to order as suggested in many a restaurant. Every food has its optimum degree of cooking.

Of all the mistakes we are likely to encounter in restaurants or make ourselves at home, most involve doneness, typically overcooking. Every fish book in my library says to cook a lobster for 20 minutes; I suggest cooking it just 4 minutes. Suggestions for roast chicken and turkey say that the internal temperature should be 160°F/71°C or even more, guaranteeing that it will be overcooked. I say 140°F/60°C for a chicken or turkey. Seafood is often subjected to the horrors of too much heat for too long. Keep in mind that most seafood is best raw, but once you decide to cook it, it should not be undercooked. The flesh of a properly cooked whole fish should barely cling to the bones and be slightly pink and translucent where it attaches. Fish should not be flaky.

Once you recognize what doneness looks like (or, more likely, feels like)—and there are plenty of pictures here to help you with that—you need to think about the cooking process itself and match the correct cooking method to the food being prepared. Techniques for determining the doneness of a braise are completely different than those used for a roast; a loaf of bread requires different criteria than does a cake. You need to know the best method for getting there—high heat for roasting, low heat for braising, medium heat for baking. Some foods must be "seized" on the stove, which is to say they should sizzle when you place them in the fat. Here, I've included a number of tricks, such as taking the thighbone out of a chicken so it cooks at the same rate as a breast or grilling a fish with its scales on so it doesn't stick to the grates.

As you become a more experienced cook, determining doneness—the most difficult aspect of cooking—will become second nature and very much intuitive. One of the most difficult foods to cook properly is a large roast because it changes relatively little during the early stages of cooking. You'll learn to look at the juices it releases (as well as their color), the feel the roast should have when you press on it, and, of course, the appropriate internal temperature.

Here, cooking times have been downplayed and, in fact, are often not included at all. Since ovens are notoriously inaccurate and everyone has a different touch, it's best to work out your own cooking times from experience. It may help, for example, to determine that a turkey takes about 10 minutes per 1 lb/455 g to cook in a 350°F/175°C oven, but these are only estimates so you can organize your cooking schedule, not surefire guides to appropriate doneness.

Much of cooking is intuitive or, if not actually intuitive, based on a huge amount of sensory input. A chicken jus develops a particular smell when it reaches the exact point that it's done; a rack of lamb will stiffen in a characteristic and easy-to-measure way. Every food has its little tricks and, sometimes, subtle changes that act as clues for measuring doneness. Once these are mastered, cooking indeed becomes a joy.

HOW WE DETERMINE DONENESS

COOKING MAY BE THE ONLY ART FORM that requires all the senses. The sound of meat sizzling alerts you that the flame is hot enough; the smell of juices caramelizing tells you a roast is ready; and the texture of meat and seafood tells you, by feel, when they're done.

While determining doneness does indeed require all five senses, it is touch that is perhaps the most important. This is because we determine the doneness of many cuts of meat and fish by pressing on them and assessing their texture. Meats, and proteins in general, become firm to the touch as they cook. To get a feel for this, press on a muscle on your body that isn't flexed (the muscle on the inside of the base of the thumb is a good one; the bicep, another) and just flex the muscle. Another way to familiarize yourself with this technique for determining doneness is to cook a boneless chicken breast in a sauté pan or over a grill and then touch it as it cooks. Because chicken breasts are usually thinner at one end, you can feel the firmness start there and then work its way up to the thicker part of the breast. As soon as the entire breast springs back to the touch, it is done. Further cooking will only dry it out.

Things become a little trickier when we cook red meat because we have to cook it to varying degrees, depending on people's taste. A rare steak will feel completely fleshy, a medium-rare steak will just begin to feel slightly firm, and a medium steak is ready as soon as it feels firm like a flexed muscle. White meat—veal, pork, or chicken—is always cooked to the same degree, which is to say medium.

While the touching method is almost universally useful, it becomes more difficult when we're cooking larger cuts of meat because it is harder to get a sense of how the interior is cooking. (This is possible but it takes a lot of experience.) The obvious solution is to use an instant-read thermometer, stuck in the middle of a large piece of meat (usually a roast) and simply follow the temperature guidelines. But what if there is no thermometer around? If you're cooking a roast, as it starts to cook through you'll notice drops of blood pearling on its outer surface. When there are no juices forming, the meat is *very* rare—one could almost say raw. When the first red droplets of blood form on the roast, the roast is rare. As these juices become more copious—but remain red—the roast is medium-rare. As soon as the juices have streaks of brown in them, the roast is medium. Higher temperatures will simply cause the release of more juices. You'll be able to make an excellent jus but your meat will be dried out.

To further enhance your skills, learn the lip test. The lip test consists of inserting a metal skewer into the roast—with the tip right in the center—leaving it in the roast for about 5 seconds, and then immediately touching the tip of the skewer to your lower lip. If the skewer is cool, the roast is obviously not ready. As soon as the skewer feels neither hot nor cold, it is very rare. When it feels just warm, it is medium-rare. The best way to learn the lip test is to use an instant-read thermometer and as you take the reading,

touch it to your lip. Look at the temperature and associate the feeling with the temperature. (You can even heat some water in a saucepan to various degrees and then test it with the thermometer and lip test.) Don't listen to those who say this is unsanitary. It's only unsanitary if you reinsert the same skewer back into whatever it is you're cooking.

There is another situation that calls for a skewer or small, thin knife. When braising meat or certain seafood (octopus), the food is ready when a skewer slides easily in and out. If the food is underdone, the food will cling to the skewer. One point of confusion for many beginning cooks is the notion that internal temperature is important while braising. You can't determine if a braise (a long braise; see "Braising," page 16) is done by taking the temperature, since the temperature will already be high (around 190°F/88°C); there's no difference in temperature from beginning to end.

We also use our sense of smell to determine doneness. When caramelizing a jus, for example (see "Making Jus or Gravy," page 129), the pan is ready to be deglazed as soon as the rich and complex odor of the caramelized jus hits your nose. Artichokes are typically done when you can smell them; so are certain roasts, such as leg of lamb, which is typically cooked a little longer than beef (beef being served rare and lamb, medium-rare).

While it may come as a surprise, hearing is also important, if not for determining exactly when things are done but to determine if they're cooking properly. For example, when you're sautéing plain chicken that isn't breaded, it should make a clear sizzling sound when you place it in the hot pan. If you don't hear the sizzle, your pan isn't hot enough and the chicken may stick. You also use hearing to determine how foods are cooking in a pressure cooker—the pressure should be up but you should hear no hissing, which would indicate that the liquid is boiling and the heat too hot.

When you've been cooking a while, you'll get a sense of how long things take to be done. (The cooking times in most cookbooks are usually too long.) This is especially important with foods that give you no cues (such as hard-boiled eggs). To be successful, you must standardize everything to eliminate variables. When cooking meat, for example, let it come to room temperature before cooking. Not only does this standardize cooking times, it also allows meat to cook more evenly. When cooking eggs, there is no way to determine if an egg is done by looking at it, smelling it, hearing it, or touching it—you must rely on time. Again, the technique you use is of little importance—whether you start in boiling water or cold, or with room-temperature eggs or refrigerated eggs—but it's essential that you be consistent with technique and time.

Sautéing

When sautéing foods, you get to use all your senses. Food sizzles in a certain way in the pan, hot butter releases a characteristic aroma, foods firm up to the touch.

The purpose of sautéing is to form a flavorful crust on foods, not to seal in flavor as was once thought. The crust, because it is somewhat hard, was thought to create a seal within which gases would expand, tenderizing the food. Now, most cooks realize that it's the simple (or not so simple) action of caramelization on the surface of foods that creates intense flavor. The principle is to keep the heat at just the right temperature so the juices released by the foods immediately caramelize on the surface. If the heat is too hot, the crust will burn; if it's too low, the juices won't caramelize, and your sautéed food may end up swimming in liquid.

To create a flavorful crust, you'll need sufficient heat to caramelize savory components as they come to the surface of the food you're sautéing. If there is insufficient heat, water will exude from the food, create steam in the bottom of the pan—further impeding the formation of crust—and the food will steam instead of brown. Food that's crowded in the pan may also steam.

Various oils and fats are used for sautéing— butter, olive oil, duck fat, flavorless oil (such as canola oil), and beef fat, to name a few. Most of the time, foods are sautéed at such a high temperature that any flavor in the cooking fat will be destroyed. For this reason it is silly to use a flavorful (and expensive) oil, such as extra-virgin olive oil or butter. Keep in mind, however, that there are exceptions. Breaded foods, for example, are normally sautéed at relatively low heat (to avoid burning the breading) such that the flavor of the cooking fat is preserved.

There are a few special tips when it comes to using butter. You can use whole (stick) butter or clarified butter (see page 26). The choice will depend on what it is you're sautéing or if you're just simply too lazy to clarify butter. If, for example, you're making an omelet, you should use whole butter for its superior flavor. The butter should be heated, starting in a cold pan (if you add butter to a hot pan it will just burn) until it froths. As the froth starts to disappear, the eggs should be added.

Whole butter can also be used for breaded foods because of the lower sautéing temperature they require. On the other hand, whole butter will leave specks in the breading that can burn as the sautéing progresses. Clarified butter is a surer bet, not only because it will not leave specks, but because, if need be, you can get it hotter than whole butter without burning it.

The sautéing temperature may also depend on what kind of pan you're using. Aluminum pans are notoriously sticky and require that you heat the oil until it begins to smoke before adding foods. Stainless steel also sticks, as does tinned copper, but you don't have to get the oil as hot as you do when using aluminum. If you're using a nonstick pan, you can sauté at any temperature you want. Just don't get the pan too hot if you have a bird in the house (the fumes from the coating are toxic to birds and no doubt to us).

Determining the temperature of your oil or fat is easy. Butter has its own idiosyncrasies because of the milk solids it contains. Milk solids tend to burn at temperatures that are too low to sauté most foods. Butter should be heated until the milk solids foam and then start to coagulate. Fats other than butter are judged by how they look and smell. As they heat in the pan, they'll begin to ripple if you move the pan slightly. Often, when fats ripple, you can go ahead and add the foods to be sautéed. As the fat gets even hotter, it will start to smoke. This is a very high temperature, useful if you're sautéing with aluminum or have foods, such as mushrooms, that have a high water content. Don't allow the oil to smoke too much before you sauté or it will give your foods a burnt, acrid taste.

Foods to sauté should be completely free of moisture on the surface. Otherwise this moisture volatilizes and creates steam, which can break down any coating forming on the foods. When adding foods to a hot sauté pan (it would be very unusual to add foods to a cold sauté pan), don't add too much at once. By adding too many vegetables or chunks of meat, the foods will, again, steam. Start by heating the pan with the fat in it and, when the pan gets to the right temperature, add the foods one piece at a time. As the food begins to brown, add more food. Continue until the foods cover the pan in a single layer. When it comes time to turn over or toss foods, don't turn too many pieces over at once or you'll cool the pan and the foods will no longer brown.

There are actually two approaches and two kinds of pans used for sautéing. The French word *sauter* means, literally, "to jump." Some foods, such as mushrooms, zucchini, or potatoes, are tossed in the pan (if tossing scares you, you can also stir, but stirring can break up vegetables), while others, such as cubes of meat, are carefully turned over with tongs—ideally tongs with no teeth, which cut into the food. If you're sautéing foods by tossing, be sure to select a pan with flared sides that provide a surface you can use to toss. If you're sautéing foods that you turn over with tongs, such as cubes of meat, use a pan with straight sides, especially if you plan to make a sauce in the pan after you take the food out. (If you cook a sauce in a pan with flared sides, it will burn on the edges of the pan.)

After you've heated your cooking fat, you're ready to add foods. The foods should sizzle when hitting the pan (exceptions are breaded cutlets), indicating that the oil or fat is hot enough. You'll learn, with experience, to judge the temperature of the fat by both its appearance and the sound it makes when you add whatever it is you're sautéing. Once you've added the foods, you'll have to regulate the heat. Much of this has to do with the thickness of what you're sautéing. If you're sautéing a thin steak, for example, you'll want to start out with the highest possible heat to ensure browning. If, on the other hand, your steak is thick, the initial heat is less important; it can be lower because the steak will spend more time in the pan and have time to brown. (A thick steak, once browned, should be sautéed over low to medium heat, never high heat.) Once the browning has been completed, however, often in a minute or two for thin steaks or longer for thick ones, there is no longer a need for high heat. In fact, if you continue to cook at too high a heat, the crust will start to burn. This is where your nose comes in handy.

Chicken is cooked in ways that take into consideration the fact that it is covered with skin. Because it is already coated in fat (the skin contains enough fat to protect the meat underneath), you can get by with a lower sautéing temperature. In fact, one of the best ways to sauté chicken is in whole butter. The fat from the skin releases and mixes with the butter while the milk solids in the butter attach to the skin and leave an intense buttery flavor.

Sticking is often a problem when sautéing. To avoid it, make sure the pan is as hot as possible without burning the cooking fat. When you add foods to a hot pan, move the pan back and forth over the flame so the food moves around in the fat. Do this for 30 seconds or so and continue to agitate the pan in this way as you add more food. This is unnecessary if you're browning steaks or chops, which are hardy enough that they pull away from the pan without sticking.

To add to the confusion, certain sauced dishes are referred to as "sautés." This simply means that a sauce was made in the pan used for the sautéing. The term is often used for veal and beef and other meats that are reheated in a sauce after they are browned. The sauce is made in the pan by first discarding the fat and deglazing with flavorful ingredients such as chopped shallots or white wine. So-called sautés are contrasted with fricassees, in which the meat finishes cooking in the sauce. In a chicken fricassee, for example, the chicken is first sautéed, the pan is deglazed, and then the chicken finishes cooking in the liquid. In a sauté, on the other hand, the chicken is simply quickly reheated in the sauce immediately before serving. Another example of a sauté is beef stroganoff, which is made with naturally tender meat, not meat that has been tenderized by long cooking.

Glazing

There are a couple of methods used for leaving a shiny glaze on food. Root vegetables, such as carrots, turnips, celeriac, and small onions, are typically glazed on top of the stove, while meats are glazed in the oven.

Glazing vegetables is somewhat more complicated than roasting them. As with all braises—glazing is a kind of braise—foods are glazed in a small amount of water or broth. Usually enough liquid is added to come halfway up the vegetable, but there is no hard-and-fast rule. The important thing is that the water or broth evaporate to dryness at the same time as the vegetables are done. In this way the braising liquid, which has captured the sugars and flavors that have run out of the vegetables, forms a shiny glaze that, in turn, coats the vegetables.

When glazing vegetables, they should be cut into a shape that makes them easy to move around in the pan. In other words, if you cut your vegetables into perfect dice, they won't roll

around in the pan when you agitate it—the vegetables must have rounded corners and edges. For this reason, not just for appearance, chefs sometimes "turn" vegetables (see "Turned Vegetables," page 68). Pearl onions, of course, present no problem because they are round. Carrots, when cut into wedges, will roll around in the pan as needed. Turnips and celeriac, unless, of course, they are tiny, should be cut into sections and the edges rounded off with a sharp paring knife.

Once you have the vegetables in the right shape, you need to find the right pan—one just large enough to hold them in a single layer. Ideally, it should have sides that go straight up and down rather than flare out. (If the edges flare out, the glaze can adhere and burn.) It should be just large enough to hold the vegetables in a single layer. Add enough water or broth to come about one-third up the sides of the vegetables, and cover the vegetables with a round of parchment paper or aluminum foil or partially cover the pan. The purpose of both these approaches is to allow the braising liquid to reduce and concentrate while still trapping heat inside the pan so that the part of the vegetable that's above the surface of the liquid will continue to cook.

Vegetables can be white glazed or brown glazed. When they are white glazed, they are glazed just long enough for the braising liquid to evaporate and coat them. When they are brown glazed, they are cooked a minute or two longer so the glaze begins to form a brown crust on the bottom of the pan. By deglazing this crust with a tablespoon or two of water and using it to glaze the vegetables, you'll achieve a golden brown glaze.

Glazing meat is usually done in the oven. If you're glazing a roast, you'll need some concentrated broth (or diluted demi-glace) to brush on the roast a few minutes before it comes out of the oven. If you're glazing braised meat, such as pot roast, you'll use the braising liquid as the source for the glaze. The usual method is to transfer the meat to a clean and smaller pot and then baste it with its braising liquid in a hot oven. The braising liquid reduces to a glaze on the surface of the meat. This glaze is not only attractive, but it also creates a burst of flavor.

Braising

To put it simply, braising is cooking in a small amount of liquid. It is contrasted with poaching, in that poaching requires enough liquid to completely cover the food at hand. Large cuts are typically braised with enough liquid to come halfway up their sides, while stews are completely covered in liquid.

There are several approaches to braising. First, there is long braising and short braising. These are important distinctions because long-braised foods end up with a definite texture, one we usually associate with stew, while short-braised foods will have the same consistency as if they were roasted or sautéed. Long-braised foods are cooked at a relatively high temperature (around 190°F/88°C). They are finished when a skewer slides easily in and through the meat without gripping. Short-braised foods, on the other hand, are finished when they reach a specific internal temperature. Their doneness is judged in the same way as sautéed or roasted foods. Examples of long-braised foods are pot roasts and stews; short-braised foods include braised seafood (excluding octopus and squid), or meats that are cooked for only a few minutes, such as the beef in beef stroganoff.

Chefs also refer to brown braising and white braising. The difference has to do with whether the meat was browned or not before it came in contact with liquid. Most seafood braises are white braises, while most meat braises are brown braises. The terms have nothing to do with the color of the dish. A red wine beef stew can be a white braise if the meat is not browned before it is cooked in liquid.

Given these distinctions, keep in mind that they are used with each other. In other words, there are long brown braises, long white braises, short brown braises, and short white braises.

Long brown braising is what most of us think of when we think of braising. The aroma of a slow-cooking stew or pot roast is impossible to dissociate with long slow cooking. To make a long brown braise, the meat must first be browned, either in the oven or by sautéing in hot fat. Once browned, it is placed in a pot that fits it as closely as possible (to diminish the need for liquid). If the braise is a stew, enough liquid is added to barely cover the meat. If it's a pot roast, enough liquid should be added to come halfway up the sides of the meat. Most of the time aromatic vegetables and a bouquet garni (a bundle of herbs) are placed in the liquid. The liquid can be virtually anything—including water, or something flavorful, such as broth, wine, or cider.

Once the ingredients are in the pot, the meat is covered loosely with a sheet of aluminum foil large enough to cover the top of the pot. The foil is then pressed over the meat such that any liquid condensing on the foil will drip down and baste the roast. If you're lucky enough to have one of those special pots with stalactite-like spikes that hang down from the underside of the lid, you can skip the foil. When the meat has cooked for an hour or two (it will depend on the meat) over a tiny flame or in a low oven, the meat that was submerged in liquid will have cooked more completely than that which was above. Turn the meat over so that the part that was submerged is now protruding above the surface. Continue braising until a skewer penetrates the meat without any resistance. If you're cooking a stew, you obviously won't have to worry about turning the meat because it is completely submerged in liquid. A stew is done when you can easily crush a piece of meat between two fingers.

If you've made a stew, you'll need to think about the braising liquid—if it needs thickening, reducing, or nothing at all. You may want to thicken it with beurre manié (a paste of flour and butter), cornstarch, or vegetable purée. You may want to simmer down the braising liquid to concentrate its flavor.

If you've made a braised pot roast, there are a couple more steps. The meat should be transferred to a smaller pot just large enough to hold it. The braising liquid should be reduced by half on the stove while being carefully degreased, and then poured over the meat. The meat should be cooked in a moderate to hot oven, uncovered, while basting every 5 minutes with the braising liquid. As you continue with this glazing, the braising liquid will reduce into an intensely flavored sauce and the roast will be covered with a shiny red glaze.

Short brown braising might be as simple as a sauté that you finish with liquid. In other words, you may sauté a thick pork chop and decide that the crust will be too tough if you rely on sautéing alone to cook the meat through. So you add a little wine and perhaps a little broth and finish cooking the chop in a covered pan. Chicken is often cooked in this way—lightly browned in fat, fat discarded, liquid such as broth added, and the chicken gently simmered until done.

Long white braising simply means that whatever it is you're braising was not first browned. An example might be a meat stew in which the meat was simply covered with liquid before braising. This is a great trick to know—you don't have to perform the messy job of browning the meat to make a good stew.

Short white braising is often used for fish. The fish, usually fillets, is placed in a pan with enough liquid to come halfway up the pan's sides. The pan is heated on the stove, the whole thing loosely covered with foil, and slid into the oven. Once done, the fish is transferred to plates or a platter and a sauce is made with the braising liquid. At times the fish is glazed under the broiler after being coated with the thickened braising liquid.

Braising with a Pressure Cooker

Pressure cookers cook in less time because water boils at a higher temperature when under pressure. Remember, when braising (or poaching) it's essential that the liquid does not boil. I've always avoided the pressure cooker for braising because I assumed that it would heat the liquid too hot, causing the liquid to cloud. But there's a trick for avoiding this: Don't heat the pressure cooker to the point when steam starts shooting out of the safety valve. In other words, if you hear it hissing, turn it down. If you let the pressure cooker heat just enough to keep up the pressure but not to cause the safety valve to hiss, you'll end up with golden brown, clear braising liquid that looks a little like bourbon whiskey.

Determining when foods are done in a pressure cooker can only be managed by the length of cooking time. Some pressure cookers have more than one setting for pressure, making a standard recipe hard to follow. In general, a pressure cooker cooks in half the time (however, when set to the highest pressure, mine cooks even faster), but until you get used to using it, I would suggest experimenting with something like a stew and then checking its doneness every 15 minutes or so.

Frying

Unfairly maligned, frying seals in the flavor of foods like no other technique. To be successful, fried foods are best served right out of the fryer—in fact, it's better to have people standing around the kitchen as you fish foods from the pot than it is to have them in the dining room.

Cooks divide frying into deep-frying and shallow-frying. When deep-frying, the food is totally submerged in fat; when shallow-frying, the fat comes about halfway up whatever it is that's being fried. Both techniques are approached in a similar way.

Keep in mind that frying is dangerous. Don't ever fill a pot more than halfway with oil or it might overflow (it might overflow anyway); fry on a back burner, where there's less chance of someone accidentally bumping the pot. Have a box of baking powder on hand to pour over any fires that might occur if the oil overflows. Add foods slowly, or a few at a time, until you can judge how much the oil is going to froth up. Always use a spider or skimmer or some other implement, such as a slotted spoon, to lower the foods into the oil. If you use your fingers, the oil can splash and leave you with a nasty burn.

One of the reasons frying is dangerous is that the oil is heated until it's much hotter than boiling water—usually around 350°F/175°F. The exact temperature of the oil depends on the size of what is being fried. Small objects—say, slices of zucchini—should be fried using very high heat so they brown quickly and don't have a chance to become soggy. Larger foods, such as chicken, need to be fried at a lower temperature so they don't brown too much by the time they cook through.

Foods can be fried just as they are or they can be coated with a batter. There is much debate as to what makes the best batter, and recipes range from a simple dusting of flour (my favorite for chicken) to batters containing eggs and beer. The batter should be thin and light so it doesn't absorb too much oil.

Most frying these days is done in vegetable oil, which has a fairly high smoking temperature and doesn't introduce any cholesterol. Unfortunately, vegetable oil doesn't have much of a taste. I prefer frying in "pure" olive oil, which is at least a grade down from extra-virgin. Don't use extra-virgin olive oil because the heat will destroy its delicacy. The best fat for frying is suet, which is rendered beef kidney fat. To make suet (it used to be you could buy it from a butcher, but those days have passed), buy the white brittle fat that surrounds the kidneys on a steer. (You'll need to special order this from your butcher.) Cut the fat up into chunks and slowly render it in a heavy-bottomed pot. When the chunks turn into cracklings, strain the fat and use it for frying (see photos, page 60).

Roasting

Originally, *roasting* meant to cook on a spit in front of a roaring fire. The spit would rotate so the food cooked evenly. A pan placed under the food would catch the juices. One of the great advantages of this method was that the roast was exposed to the open air. Because of this, there was no humidity to slow down the browning and crisping process. Given this, stovetop spits or spits that fit in the oven may help a roast to brown evenly but they won't emulate the effects of authentic roasting because humidity will still be trapped inside with the roast. The roast may also pick up smells from the oven or from its own burning fat.

Nowadays we roast in an oven. Typically the roast is placed on a bed of aromatic vegetables and extra pieces of meat to provide juices for the jus or gravy. This not only helps make the jus but keeps the roast from sticking to the pan.

Roasting presents an exercise in controlled browning. Much like sautéed or grilled foods, the heat of the oven must be adjusted so the roast is properly browned at the same time it is done. There are a number of approaches to achieve this. One method, commonly used in restaurants, is to cook the roast with high heat to brown it and then turn the oven down to the desired internal temperature, say 125°F/52°C, to finish cooking over a period of up to 24 hours. This doesn't work at home because our ovens aren't accurate enough and don't go to a low enough temperature.

A good approach for the home cook is to start the roast in a hot oven—500°F/260°C—until it browns and then reduce the oven's temperature to a point at which the roast will continue to cook but not brown any further.

Keep in mind that the smaller the roast, the higher the oven temperature should be. This is to ensure that the roast browns before it overcooks. Some roasts are too small to brown in the oven in the required time and should be browned on the stovetop before being slid into the oven. Such things as quail fit into this category.

Most people buy roasting pans that are too large, maybe good for the Thanksgiving turkey but not for much else. The roasting pan should fit the size of the roast and have a heavy bottom so any areas not covered by the roast don't burn. I especially like oval copper gratin pans. Because copper is such a good conductor of heat, the gratin pans never burn despite not being as thick as they should be. Cast-iron pans also make good roasting pans—they're nice and heavy—but they have the disadvantage of being black. When juices caramelize on a black surface they are impossible to see and assess.

The bottom of the roasting pan should be covered with aromatic vegetables such as onions, carrots, or turnips. The vegetables should be cut according to the predicted roasting time—the shorter the roasting time, the smaller the cut. This is so the vegetables finish cooking at the same time as the roast. The layer of vegetables can be as simple as a sliced onion or a more complex mirepoix (a mixture of chopped carrots, onions, and a little celery), or even one containing cured ham such as prosciutto (buy the end pieces—they're cheaper). Meat can also be added to this layer to provide extra juices. A roast chicken, for example, might have a small sliced carrot, a coarsely chopped half onion, and perhaps half a turnip cut into medium dice. In addition, 1 lb/455 g or so of chicken drumsticks can be hacked up with a cleaver and used for this roasting pan base.

The purpose of the roasting pan base, other than keeping the roasting pan from sticking to the roast, is to provide flavorful juices that mingle with those from the roast. Ideally, the base of vegetables and meat should finish cooking at the same time as the roast, but if it doesn't, this is easy to control. If you take the roast out of the oven and find that the base hasn't cooked, just slide the pan into the oven and continue roasting until the vegetables and meat release juices that caramelize on the bottom of the pan. You can also pre-roast the base by giving it 15 minutes or so in a hot oven before placing the roast on top.

Once the roast comes out of the oven, it's time to make a jus or gravy (a gravy is just a thickened jus; see "Making Jus or Gravy," page 129).

Poaching

Poaching differs from braising in that the foods are completely submerged in the cooking liquid. Much of the time the poaching liquid is not served, but it's still imperative that it have a good flavor so that it scents the foods being poached.

The most famous poached meat dish, in French cooking at least, is the pot-au-feu. A pot-au-feu is a collection of tough cuts of beef that are gently simmered in water or broth until tender. The broth is then served, with little cheese croutons, as the first course, followed by the meat. The meat is accompanied by coarse salt, mustard, and sometimes tomato sauce. A similar dish is the *bollito misto*. A bollito misto is similar to a pot-au-feu except that a larger variety of meats—often from different animals—is used. The accompaniments are also different and include a tartarlike green sauce and a sweet fruit sauce called *mostarda di Cremona*.

When poaching meat, it's best to use tough cuts—the same cuts you would use for braising—that will break down and soften during the slow poaching. It's best to start with cold water and gently heat the liquid until it comes to a bare simmer. It should never boil. Starting in cold liquid causes certain proteins in the meat to release into the poaching liquid, where they float to the top and can be easily skimmed off. If the meat is added to hot liquid, the proteins released are very fine and will cloud the broth. At times, however, it's necessary to add meats to hot liquid—meats that cook more quickly, such as chicken, duck, and tender cuts of beef.

Some recipes call for poaching tender cuts of meat that we normally associate with roasting. For example, in a *boeuf à la ficelle*, a beef tenderloin is poached in the pot-au-feu liquid (or just broth) for a very short time and is then served rare. Duck breast also takes well to this treatment, but the skin should be sautéed for several minutes first to render the fat. You can also poach a chicken in the pot-au-feu, keeping in mind the cooking time (about 45 minutes).

Pot-au-feu variations can be elaborate to the point of ridiculousness. In one such version, a consommé—a perfectly clear broth—is prepared with oxtail and short ribs. This consommé is then used to poach a whole foie gras, a capon breast studded with truffles, and a beef tenderloin.

Some chefs have taken the pot-au-feu theme and made a number of exciting derivatives. For example, a petite marmite contains various meats surrounded with consommé. Michel Guérard's seafood pot-au-feu isn't really a pot-au-feu since all the fish are not poached but are cooked using different methods and then served together, surrounded with broth.

Poaching is really the same as making broth except that the emphasis is on the solids in the broth instead of on the broth itself. For example, one might poach a hen (*poule au pot*) in chicken broth or water with the goal of eating the hen. In this case, the hen should be added to the cold broth or water and the liquid then slowly heated until it reaches a slow simmer.

Seafood also takes very well to poaching. Usually it is poached in a court bouillon (a vegetable broth) and can be served surrounded with its poaching liquid. One good trick when making the court bouillon is to julienne the vegetables and leave them in the broth. The seafood can then be served with the julienned vegetables in a tangle on top and around. When the vegetables in the court bouillon are left in and served this way, the dish is referred to as *à la nage*. Cooking à la nage is perfect for shellfish such as scallops and crayfish (served whole in the shells).

Poaching whole fish poses the problem of which vessel to use for the poaching. The best solution for roundfish is a fish poacher, which is essentially a long pot with a rack in it for pulling the fish out of the poaching liquid once it is done. Flatfish pose another set of problems. Ideally, they should be poached in a diamond-shaped fish poacher (see page 117), also with a rack, called a *turbotière*.

We also poach vegetables such as beets or other root vegetables by simmering them in liquid until done. When making a court bouillon we're also poaching vegetables, except that the vegetables are usually discarded and it's the broth we want.

Grilling

While roasting occurs in front of the heat and broiling below, grilling occurs directly *over* the heat source.

The grill temperature should be adjusted according to the thickness of the foods being grilled. The thicker the foods, the farther they should be from the heat source and the lower the heat should be. (The heat can be reduced on a charcoal grill by putting on the cover for a couple of minutes.) If you have a thin piece of fish, meat, or vegetable, get the grill as hot as possible so a nice brown crust will form before the food overcooks.

There is one primary problem that occurs while grilling and that is the tendency of foods to drip fat down on the coals and cause flare-ups.

Now, some of us like the bitter flavor of steaks that have been charred around the edges, but in general, try to prevent flames from touching the meat or they'll leave a sooty taste.

Classic grilling occurs uncovered, but modern grills often have covers. Using the cover slows down the heat by starving the coals of oxygen and can actually cause foods to smoke. But there is an advantage to using the cover, especially for thick pieces of meat or fish, which must be grilled at a relatively low temperature. If the fire is built to one side of the grill, the foods can be browned on one side of the grill—over the coals—and then moved away from the coals to keep cooking without direct exposure to the heat source, which can cause the foods to get too brown.

To avoid flare-ups you may need to move the foods around as flames occur. Don't put a lot of oil on your food—wipe off any oily marinade—or it will drip down under the grill and cause a flare-up. If you're using a charcoal grill for grilling chicken, grill on the flesh side first so that by the time you cook on the skin side—it's the skin that releases fat and causes flames—the fire has died down somewhat.

Broiling

While grilling is cooking with the heat source below the food, broiling happens when the heat source is *above* the food. The effect is similar to grilling except, of course, no woody flavor is imparted.

One of the major problems with broilers is they're not hot enough. To deal with this it's often necessary to get the food very close to the heat source—within 1 in/2.5 cm or so—and then watch it like a hawk. If you're broiling a thick steak, this is less critical since there will be time for the meat to brown before it overcooks. But if you're browning something thin, then the food should be as close to the heat source as possible.

It doesn't help that most home broilers are beneath the oven, next to the floor. The only way to deal with this is to lie down on the floor so you can watch the broiling.

Smoking

Many of us forget about smoking because we assume it's complicated or, at the very least, that it will smoke up our house.

Keep in mind that there are two kinds of smoking: hot and cold. When foods are hot-smoked, the smoke is hot enough to cook the foods. When foods are cold-smoked, the foods are kept sufficiently far away from the heat source so they don't cook. An example of a cold-smoked food is smoked salmon, which is cured, but not cooked.

Hot-smoking is far easier to perform in a home kitchen than cold-smoking. While you can buy a hot smoker that fits over the stove, it's easy to make one yourself. Take a round cake rack and cut it as needed so it fits in a wok or in a heavy iron skillet. Put a tablespoon or so of sawdust or wood chips in the bottom of the wok or skillet,

cover the sawdust with a small sheet of aluminum foil, and heat over high heat until the wood starts to smoke. Place the food on the cake rack and cover the wok or skillet. Time the smoking as you would a roast.

Cold-smoking is another matter altogether. You'll first need a heat source and then some kind of container to hold whatever it is you're smoking. The container should be far enough away from the heat source so that the smoke is cool. To smoke a whole salmon fillet, first cure the salmon with a mixture of sugar and salt (¼ cup/32 g sugar for every 1 cup/128 g salt) for two to three days before wiping the cure off the fish and putting the fish in the smoker.

Barbecuing

Often confused with plain grilling, barbecuing involves a whole different process. While there is a huge variety of barbecue styles, the principle remains the same. Meat is marinated and then slowly cooked in a covered grill while being periodically brushed with sauce. This results in a process that combines braising and smoking. The braising occurs because the meat is in contact with liquid and heat; the smoking occurs simply as a result of using flavorful wood chips or sawdust as the heat source.

SAUCES

Clarified Butter

In addition to containing butterfat, which is golden and transparent when warm, butter contains about 25 percent water and 5 percent proteins. The proteins burn at relatively low temperatures, which can sometimes pose a problem because it means we can't use very high heat to sauté with butter unless we remove the milk solids (the proteins).

To eliminate the water and the proteins, we clarify butter by slowly cooking it until the milk solids coagulate and are strained off or we simply melt the butter and skim off the milk solids. There are two ways to do this: the restaurant method, for 5 lb/2.3 kg or more of butter, and the home method, for less than that. The restaurant method is the simplest and makes sense for larger amounts. Just melt the butter in a pot, skim off and discard the frothy milk solids that float to the top, and then scoop out the golden liquid butterfat. The water will be left sitting on the bottom of the pot. Clarified butter keeps in the refrigerator for up to 6 months when stored in a tightly sealed container to protect it from absorbing odors.

The home method consists of cooking the butter down until the milk solids coagulate and caramelize and can be strained out. This also gives the butter a distinctly nutty taste. Butter cooked in this way is also called *ghee* or *beurre noisette*.

[1] To make clarified butter using the home method, bring 5 lb/2.3 kg or less of unsalted butter to a boil, generating a lot of froth. [2] As the butter cooks, the froth will die down. [3] As it continues to cook, the butter will start to froth again and the milk solids will start to attach to the sides of the pan. [4] When the sides and bottom of the pan are covered with brown coagulated milk solids, dip the bottom of the pan into a bowl of cold water to stop the cooking. [5] When it cools off for a few seconds, you will see golden fat with a little froth on top. [6] Strain the butter through a fine-mesh strainer. When the butter has cooled to room temperature, transfer it to a glass jar with a tight-fitting lid and refrigerate.

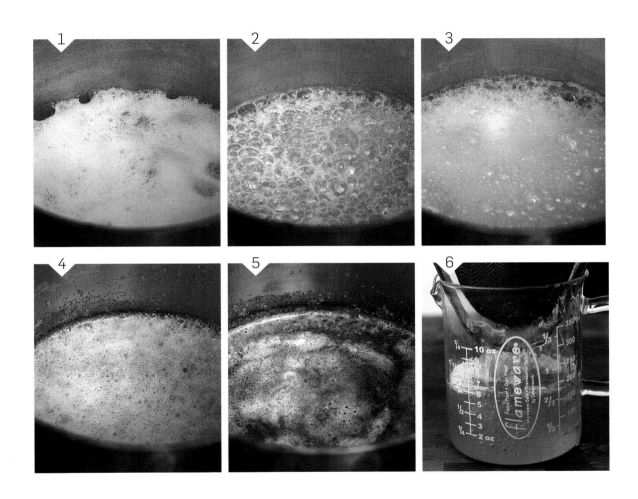

Mayonnaise and Aïoli

A classic mayonnaise is made by slowly working vegetable oil into an egg yolk (or yolks). Usually some mustard and lemon juice are also added. If you're making a classic mayonnaise, with vegetable oil, it can be made in a blender or food processor.

The stumbling block for most cooks is the tendency of mayonnaise to break, which means it suddenly separates and liquefies. This happens if the oil is added too quickly to the egg yolk; the two will never emulsify. To avoid this, the oil must be added very slowly, especially at the beginning. Don't add the oil in a steady stream—at least not at the beginning—or you'll be adding it too fast. Instead, work the oil in a teaspoon at a time. As the oil is incorporated and the mayonnaise starts to thicken, add the oil a tablespoon at a time. When the mayonnaise continues to get thicker, add the oil in a thin stream down the side of the bowl. You may also need to add a teaspoon or so of lemon juice or water to thin it just a little if becomes too thick. A mayonnaise that is too thick can break because the microscopic globules of oil are forced together rather than truly binding.

One good trick for those new to making mayonnaise: Add a spoonful of bottled mayonnaise to kick-start your mixture. That way it won't be up to you to establish the emulsion of the oil and egg yolks, because the bottled mayonnaise is already an emulsion.

An old-fashioned aïoli is mayonnaise made with garlic and extra-virgin olive oil. The garlic is worked to a paste in a mortar, and the oil is added in dribbles until the whole thing holds together in a pale yellow emulsion. The oil must be worked in by hand because the rapid movement of a blender will turn it bitter. If you don't have a mortar and pestle, just crush the chopped garlic with the side of a knife and mix everything in a nonmetal mixing bowl.

[1] To make aïoli, grind garlic cloves to a paste in a mortar or by working them to a paste with the side of a knife. [2] Work in an egg yolk or more as needed. [3] Slowly work in vegetable oil (you can make the aïoli using only extra-virgin olive oil but it will be very strong tasting) until the aïoli just starts to thicken. [4] Finish the aïoli by stirring in extra-virgin olive oil. [5] The aïoli is finished when it is thick and can stay in a mound on the pestle. [6] Don't add the oil too quickly. [7] Adding the oil too quickly results in a broken, or separated and not emulsified, aïoli.

Continued >>

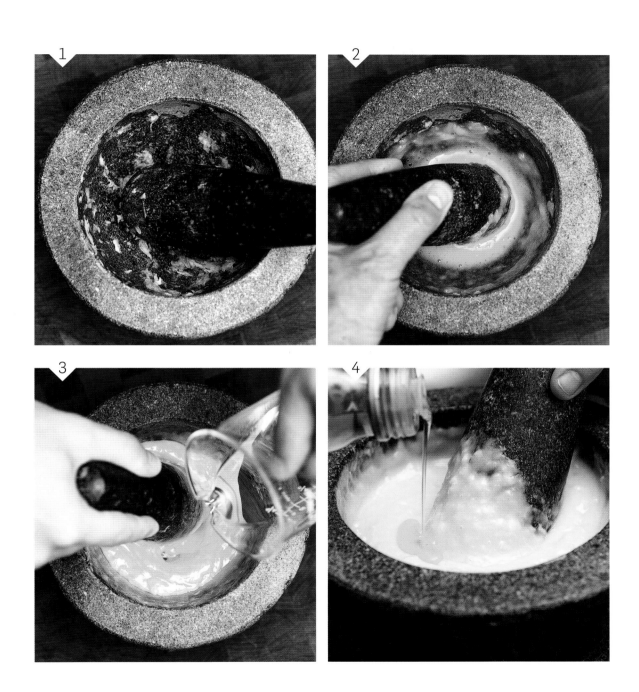

Emulsions Explained

When two mutually insoluble liquids need to be mixed, they must be combined in an emulsion. For example, when you make a vinaigrette, if you simply combine the ingredients and shake the jar, the oil and vinegar will never come together; they will separate and the oil will float on top. This is because they are not emulsified.

An emulsion consists of microscopic droplets, usually of fat, surrounded with liquid such as water, lemon juice, vinegar, or wine. A mayonnaise, for example, is made of infinitesimally small droplets of oil surrounded by a small amount of liquid such as lemon juice. A beurre blanc or hollandaise is similar—droplets of melted butter are surrounded with a solution of wine and vinegar.

So how do we create such an emulsion? First, an emulsion requires an emulsifier. An emulsifier is usually a protein such as egg yolk, mustard, the milk solids in butter, or heavy cream. The protein molecules in an emulsifier are soluble on one end in fat, and on the other end in liquid such as wine, water, or lemon juice, with the net result that the tiny particles of liquid or fat become surrounded with molecules, half immersed in the particle, half protruding out into the surrounding liquid. Imagine a sphere with lots of pointy molecules sticking out of it. These molecules keep the globules from touching each other and coalescing into larger droplets, which would cause the mixture to separate (or break).

Once you can visualize this, it's easy to imagine how an emulsion breaks. If it gets too hot, the molecules of the emulsifier can become denatured, which is to say broken up so they no longer perform their function. Emulsions can also break if they become too thick—in other words, there is too little liquid surrounding the globules, forcing them together and causing them to coalesce. Using too little emulsifier will also cause the emulsion to break, but keep in mind that an egg yolk is a very powerful emulsifier—one egg yolk will set at least 1 qt/950 ml of oil (even though we usually use a higher proportion of egg yolks to oil than this).

Hollandaise Sauce

Few sauces are guaranteed to intimidate cooks as much as hollandaise sauce. This is no doubt because of the sauce's tendency to break at the slightest provocation. It's also easy to curdle the sauce by applying too much heat.

Hollandaise is made much like a mayonnaise—by slowly working fat into egg yolks—except that instead of oil, melted butter (or even better, clarified butter) is beaten into the egg yolks. There is another significant difference: When making mayonnaise, the oil must be added very slowly to form an emulsion. An emulsion is a kind of mixture that combines liquids and fats that normally wouldn't mix (see "Emulsions Explained," page 31). With hollandaise, the emulsion is established before adding any butter by beating the egg yolks with air and water. Once this emulsion is established, the butter can be added relatively quickly.

One common mistake is clarifying butter just before making the hollandaise and then not letting the clarified butter cool enough before adding it to the beaten egg yolks. Keep in mind that hollandaise is a warm sauce, not a hot one. If your hollandaise does suddenly liquefy and separate, indicating that it has broken, make a new emulsion (in this case, a sabayon) by beating an egg yolk with a tablespoon of water over low heat and then, off the heat, whisk the broken hollandaise into the new sabayon. There are a number of factors that cause a hollandaise to break: the butter is too hot, you've added it too quickly, or you've added too much butter for the number of yolks. The egg yolks in a hollandaise sauce can take on a lot of butter. I usually think in terms of a stick of butter per egg yolk—a classic hollandaise is mostly butter—but the amount can also be made much smaller, depending on your preference.

[1] To make a hollandaise, combine 4 egg yolks with 4 tablespoons of cold water in a heavy-bottomed saucepan, preferably one with sloping sides that allow the whisk to reach into the corners of the pan where the yolk could accumulate and curdle. [2] Whisk over medium heat until frothy. Watch carefully as you whisk the yolks and don't allow them to get too hot, which will cause them to curdle. [3] As soon as you can see the bottom of the pan while you're whisking, the initial emulsion is ready. [4] Add 1 cup/240 ml or more (up to 4 cups/950 ml) melted or clarified butter in a thin but steady stream while whisking. [5] The finished sauce will look thick, almost like mayonnaise. However, if you made your hollandaise with whole butter (which contains water), the sauce will be thinner.

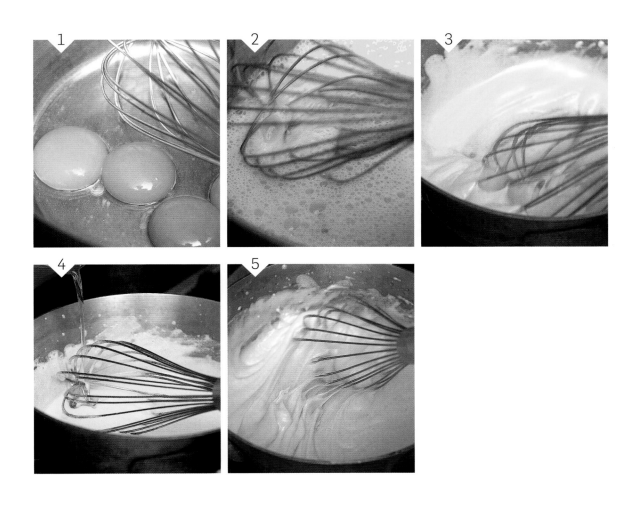

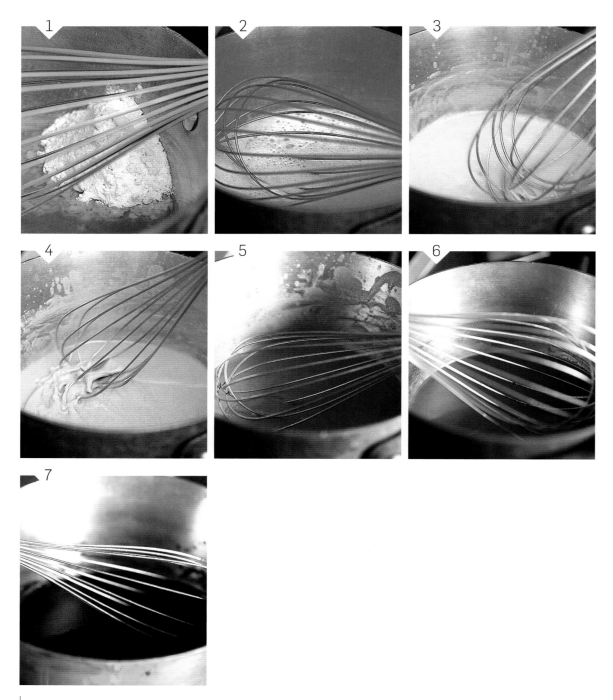

Roux

A roux is a thickener for liquids such as milk or broth. It's a mixture of equal parts fat and flour, cooked over low to medium heat to different degrees of doneness, depending on its intended use. White roux, the most common, is simply cooked for a minute or two until the flour smells toasty. A blond roux takes on a beige appearance and has a nutty flavor. Brown roux, used for making brown sauces, is a deep chestnut color. Creole cooking uses a roux that's cooked until it's almost black.

The fat you use will depend on how you're going to use the roux. Butter is the most commonly used fat for roux but will burn and leave specks in the roux if cooked for a long time, as for a brown roux. For this reason, if you want to use butter, it should be clarified unless you're making a white roux. If you don't have butter, or have some aversion to it, feel free to use other fats, such as rendered chicken or duck fat, pork fat, olive oil, or vegetable oil.

[1] To make a roux, combine equal parts of flour and fat over medium heat. [2] Whisk until the flour turns frothy. [3] After about 2 minutes of cooking, the white roux will smell toasty. [4] When cooked for about 6 minutes, you will have a blond roux. [5] After 10 minutes, it will become a brown roux. [6] A dark brown roux, used for gumbos and other Creole dishes, is cooked for about 20 minutes. [7] A burnt roux will appear grainy and almost black.

Salad Vinaigrette

For something so simple, vinaigrette stumps a lot of beginning cooks and, for that matter, advanced cooks. Vinaigrette is an emulsion similar to mayonnaise—hence its unpredictability—but instead of an egg yolk being used as the emulsifier, mustard is used. Much in the style of a mayonnaise, the mustard is beaten with a little vinegar and then oil is slowly worked in.

A classic vinaigrette is a combination of oil, vinegar, and mustard, but it also lends itself to all sorts of variations. First, you can try a different kind of mustard; the choice, of course, is up to you. You can also add herbs such as chives or tarragon. Infused vinegars and oils make exciting variations. You may want to try substituting nut oils such as walnut or hazelnut for some or all of the vegetable oil. Although many cooks like to use olive oil in their vinaigrettes, brisk whisking can cause it to turn bitter; some also think it clashes with mustard and prefer a less assertive-tasting oil.

[1] To make a vinaigrette, whisk together vinegar and mustard. [2] Whisk until smooth. [3] Pour about a tablespoon of oil down the side of the bowl. [4] Don't work the oil into the mustard mixture all at once; work it in a little bit at a time. This will prevent the vinaigrette from breaking. [5] If you add the oil too fast or you add too much, the dressing will break, or separate. [6] The vinaigrette is finished when the mixture is smooth and homogenous.

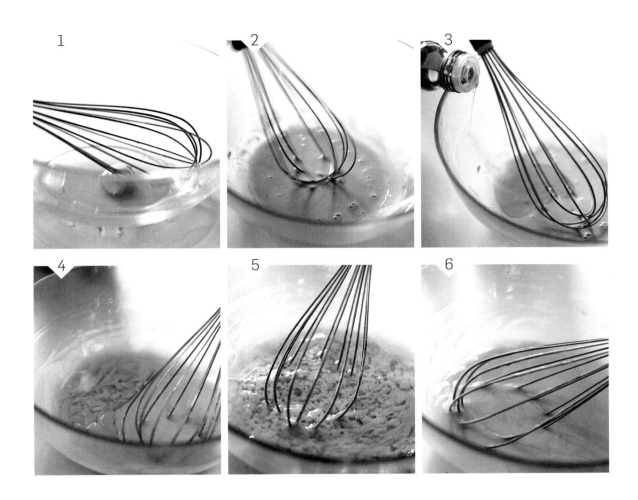

EGGS

Beaten Egg Whites

Many recipes for mousses, soufflés, and cakes call for beaten egg whites. Depending on the recipe, the whites are beaten to varying degrees.

Much has been said about the advantages of beating egg whites in a copper bowl. It is true that egg whites beaten in clean copper bowls have less of a tendency to break apart when they're allowed to sit a minute. (Although, beaten egg whites really should be used immediately after beating.) Egg whites beaten in a copper bowl are also more stable, which means that soufflés made with them are less likely to fall. However, if you don't have a copper bowl, or prefer to use your stand mixer, add a pinch of cream of tartar (or a few drops of lemon juice) to the egg whites before beating. Regardless of the equipment you're using, always include a pinch of salt, which stabilizes the beaten eggs and makes them less likely to fall as they sit. Egg whites can also be beaten with an electric mixer on high speed. If you plan to beat a lot of egg whites, buy a copper bowl that fits your mixer.

[1] While holding the whisk straight, spin it quickly between your hands to break up the whites before you begin whipping them. [2] Egg whites that have been too lightly beaten will still be liquidlike and will not hold a shape. [3] When the egg whites start to cling to the whisk, yet droop when the whisk is held sideways, they are at the soft-peak stage. [4] When the egg whites stiffen and cling to the whisk, yet sag a bit, they are at the medium-peak stage. [5] When the egg whites stick straight out from the whisk they are at the stiff-peak stage.

Hard-Boiled Eggs

Amateurs and professionals alike love to argue about how best to boil an egg. They debate whether one should start in cold water or hot, whether the eggs should be allowed to boil, whether the eggshells should be poked with a pin—the list goes on.

I prefer to start the eggs in simmering water because it causes the whites to cook before the yolks. But the choice between hot or cold isn't so much because the eggs cook any better one way or another, but because the timing is more consistent. If you start in cold water, there will be variations in how hot the stove is and how much water you're using so that the egg cooking times will never be the same. But whatever method you use, the important thing is to remain consistent. This way, you can establish your own reliable cooking times using your own method. This is essential since eggs in the shell give no indication of when they are done.

I never let the eggs actually come to a hard boil, because this level of heat is too extreme for such a delicate food and can make the cooked egg slightly tough. I also poke a tiny hole in the rounder end of the egg with a pin. This allows the air trapped in the egg to escape as it expands instead of expanding within the egg and cracking the shell.

The process is simple. Bring a big pot of water to the boil. Be sure to use at least several quarts/litres so the water keeps simmering immediately after you add the eggs. Here, the simmering times are based on taking cold eggs out of the refrigerator. If your eggs have first warmed to room temperature, the times may be shorter by a minute or two.

[1] A 2-minute egg will be completely liquid. [2] A 4-minute egg will have a runny yolk but one that has taken on a syrupy consistency. The white will be partially set. [3] A 5-minute egg shows the white completely set and the yolk beginning to set and adhere to the white. [4] A 6-minute egg has a yolk that has completely set but that is still semisolid and a shiny bright yellow-orange in color. [5] A 7-minute egg has a completely set yolk that starts to turn opaque near where it touches the white. [6] An 8-minute egg is completely set. The yolk shows opacity, mixed with sheen. [7] A 10-minute egg appears completely set. [8] A 15-minute egg will have a gray-tinged yolk and a strong sulfurous odor.

Poached Eggs

Some of us were taught to poach eggs by swirling water in a circle to make a vortex and then cracking the egg into the vortex, the idea being that this helps the egg hold together better. Instead, the outer part of the egg white—the amorphous white with no flavor—ends up coiled around the rest of the egg. This method also only allows one egg to be poached at a time. To avoid this and to work more efficiently, simply crack the eggs into a shallow pan filled three-quarters full with water—the water should be no less than 3 in/7.5 cm deep—set over medium heat. The water should be barely simmering when you crack in the egg and should maintain the slightest simmer. (If you accidentally let the water boil, it will rip apart the egg.)

As the water simmers, the egg will set and sink to the bottom. During this stage, notice the condition of the white; it should form firmly around the yolk. Don't try to lift the egg out of the water before it has had a minute or two to set or you'll tear the underside of the yolk and destroy the egg. [1] When the white becomes opaque and the egg appears firm, after about 3 minutes, lift it out with a skimmer or slotted spoon. Touch the egg white to make sure it has firmed up and touch the yolk to confirm it is still liquid. [2] Use a small paring knife to cut away the amorphous white that forms around the yolk, leaving a neat oval. [3] A properly cooked egg has a firm white and a runny yolk. [4] For those who like their poached eggs cooked longer, the egg can be cooked until the yolk is completely set, but notice that the yolk is still shiny and moist. [5] The egg can also be cooked until the egg yolk is very firm and dry.

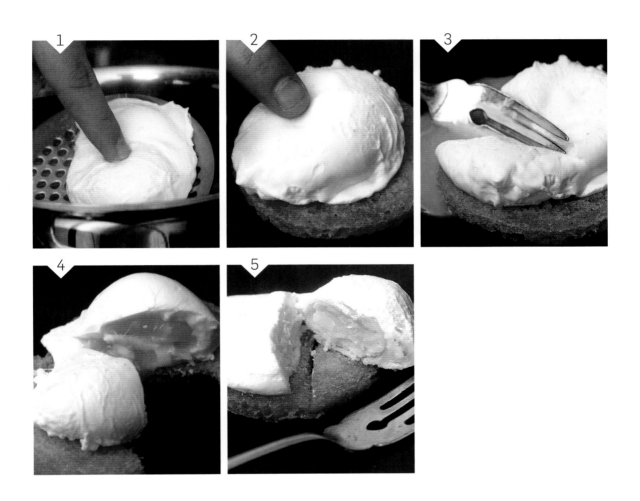

Omelets

Why omelets put the fear of God into the most intrepid cooks, I don't know. However, it must be said that there is a knack to making them. To get the knack, though, all it takes is a couple of dozen eggs and a little time to clean up the floor as you practice folding and transferring omelets from pan to plate.

Before you make your omelet, warm the eggs, still in their shells, in a bowl of warm water. This is so they cool down the pan less when they first come into contact with it. I like to add a tablespoon or two of heavy cream to the eggs to keep the omelet tender. A teaspoon of mustard helps wake up the flavor without tasting too strong.

While it's really impossible to describe making an omelet—pictures are essential—there are a few tricks to keep in mind. Give some thought to your pan. Nonstick is ideal since sticking is the bane of many an omelet maker. You can also use cast iron, provided that it has been well seasoned with oil and salt. Use whole butter for its superior flavor. Put the butter in a room-temperature pan and heat it over high heat. Swirl the pan around so the butter melts evenly. You'll notice the butter starting to froth as the pan gets hot. Once the froth begins to recede, pour in the eggs.

With the pan still over high heat, stir the eggs with the back of a fork, as though you are making scrambled eggs. Once about half the eggs have set, let the eggs congeal in a layer on the bottom of the pan. At this point, avoid cutting through the thin layer of cooked egg that forms on the bottom of the pan. [1] When all the egg has set, it's time to fold the omelet. Tilt the pan by raising the handle and banging on the handle with your fist. This will cause the far side of the omelet to ride up on the lip of the pan and fold over on itself. [2] Tilt the omelet out of the pan onto a plate and use the lip of the pan to finish folding the omelet.

[3] Most omelets you're likely to encounter in American restaurants are cooked through with no runny egg inside. [4] In other places, such as France, many people prefer the inside a little runny.

Cheese Soufflé

People are terribly intimidated by soufflés. Fearful that a soufflé will fall at the slightest provocation, cooks tiptoe around the kitchen and barely raise their voices. All this is unnecessary, since soufflés don't fall unless they've been overcooked.

Always place the soufflé dish(es) on a baking sheet so you can easily test for doneness during baking and in case of overflows. This way it won't make a mess in your oven. (But overflowing shouldn't be a problem unless your oven is too hot.)

So how does one avoid overcooking a soufflé? Since oven temperatures are notoriously unreliable and soufflé dishes come in all sizes and dimensions, it's impossible to give a predictable baking time, as can be done for a cake. There is a technique for determining doneness without cutting into the soufflé. When the soufflé has risen about 50 percent—in other words, it is 1½ times its original volume—gently move the baking sheet back and forth while watching the soufflé. When a soufflé is underdone, you'll see it move within its dish as you move the baking sheet. As the egg stiffens, the soufflé will hold still when you move the baking sheet. The goal is to remove the soufflé from the oven at exactly the point at which the eggs just start to stiffen, best assessed by gently moving the baking sheet.

When baking a soufflé, it's better to err on the side of undercooking. If it's undercooked (too "wet" looking) when you bring it to the table, you can always just stick it back in the oven—soufflés are very forgiving of brief temperature changes. On the other hand, if it's overcooked, there's not much you can do except watch it fall the minute it comes out of the oven. In fact, the French say that the inside of a soufflé should function as the sauce for the outside.

[1] An underdone soufflé will still be runny in the middle. [2] A perfectly cooked soufflé will be barely stiff. [3] When overcooked, the soufflé will have a delicious outer shell, but be nearly hollow inside.

When to Use a Collar

You'll see a lot of soufflé recipes that call for a "collar," made with aluminum foil or parchment paper. The purpose of the collar is to prevent a soufflé from overflowing as it cooks, which can happen if the dish is filled to the rim with batter. To make a collar, simply cut a strip of foil or parchment that reaches around the dish and stands 2 in/5 cm to 3 in/7.5 cm above the rim. Butter one side of the foil or parchment. Fill the dish with batter and then wrap the foil or parchment around it, buttered side in, and secure it with masking tape.

Gnocchi

While some gnocchi are made with potatoes, I prefer the texture of those made with flour, ricotta, and eggs (and in this case, spinach, too). Regardless of the dough you're working with, you know the mixture is ready to roll and cut when it's stiff enough to roll out and handle without sticking.

[1] To shape gnocchi, roll the dough into ropes about ½ in/12 mm thick. [2] Cut the gnocchi into small pillow shapes. [3] Toss the pieces into boiling water. [4] The gnocchi are done when they float to the surface. Drain the gnocchi. [5] Serve the gnocchi with broth and grated Parmigiano-Reggiano cheese.

[6] To make a gratin, top with enough cream to come about halfway up the sides of the gnocchi, but not so much that they are floating in it, and grate fontina, Gruyère, and/or Parmigiano-Reggiano over the top. Bake in a 350°F/175°C oven until browned.

Quiche Lorraine

The poor quiche has been maligned with so many baroque and unpleasant combinations—think mushrooms and broccoli—that most of us don't even remember the original version that inspired all the weird and soggy interpretations.

A quiche Lorraine is a simple custard in a crust made with bits of bacon and Gruyère cheese that are covered with a basic mixture of eggs, milk, salt, pepper, and a little nutmeg. As a rule of thumb, one large egg will set, or solidify, a filling that has ⅔ cup/165 ml of liquid, such as water, milk, stock, or a vegetable puree.

When making quiche, there are several stages at which you'll need to judge doneness. First, you need to make sure you don't overwork the dough. Second, you must judge the doneness of the pre-baked tart shell. And, last, you must judge the doneness of the quiche itself.

[1] Make the dough in a food processor, simply running the processor—there's no need for pulsing—until the dough pulls together into a ball. If it refuses to pull together, add a tablespoon of cold water and run it again. Continue in this way until the dough pulls together. If it is wet to the touch and adheres to your fingers, add ¼ cup/32 g of flour and run it again. Flatten the dough into a disk, wrap it in plastic wrap, and allow it to rest in the refrigerator for 15 minutes or so. Don't refrigerate it any longer or it will get hard and crack as you roll it.

[2] Roll out the dough and line the tart mold. [3] Pre-bake the shell (professionals call this "blind baking") by covering it with aluminum foil and then filling it with rice or beans to keep it from puffing up. Don't make the mistake of pricking the shell or the filling will leak out. Bake in a 425°F/220°C oven until the edges of the shell turn pale brown. [4] When the foil and rice or beans are removed, they should reveal a shiny, wet-looking crust. [5] Continue baking the shell until the bottom takes on a matte, pale brown appearance.

Once you have pre-baked the shell, set it on a baking sheet and sprinkle it with cooked bacon bits and grated Gruyère cheese. Cover them with a simple mixture of eggs and milk. Baking should be slow and even, so the eggs in the custard don't curdle. Bake in a low oven—about 275°F/135°C—and check the quiche after the first 20 minutes of baking. [6] To check it, gently move the baking sheet back and forth, causing the liquid in the shell to move. As you do this, you'll notice the custard first sets around the perimeter and then gradually sets more and more, moving toward the center. When you wiggle the pan and see only a small area of movement in the very center of the quiche, the quiche is done. [7] Remove from the oven and let it stand for 15 minutes before serving.

ROOTS, VEGETABLES, RICE & BEANS

Roasted or Glazed Carrots

Carrots must be cooked using a method that concentrates their flavor, namely roasting or glazing. In other words, never boil a carrot or you'll simply extract its flavor and sweetness, leaving all its natural sugars in the boiling water.

Roasting carrots is straightforward; they're simply coated with a thin layer of oil or butter (which keeps them from drying out) and roasted in a medium or hot oven (350°F/175°C to 400°F/200°C), sometimes under a joint of meat, until they are easily, but not too easily, penetrated with a skewer.

Glazing (see page 15) is more akin to braising in that it involves cooking with a small amount of liquid. Carrots have their own idiosyncrasies and are typically glazed in one of two ways. The simplest is to layer the sliced carrots in a baking dish, add enough water or broth to come one-third of the way up the sides, cover loosely with parchment paper or aluminum foil, and bake in the oven. The purpose of the parchment or foil is to trap steam that's released as the carrots glaze and at the same time allow the surrounding liquid to reduce. This ensures that those carrots that are protruding above the braising liquid are cooked at the same time as those that are submerged. To glaze using the second method, the carrots should be cut into sections, usually about 1 in/2.5 cm long. The carrot sections can be cored or even turned (see "Turned Vegetables," page 68) by carefully shaping them to resemble garlic cloves or little footballs with a small paring knife.

[1] If you're glazing sliced carrots, arrange them in a flameproof baking dish, pot, or pan, in a layer about ¾ in/2 cm thick. Don't try to make a thicker layer or they won't glaze evenly. Add enough liquid to come about one-third up the sides of the carrots (traditional recipes call for more but they leave the carrots swimming in liquid) and put the dish, pot, or pan over the stove to bring the liquid to the boil. [2] Cover loosely with parchment paper or aluminum foil. Slide the carrots into a 400°F/200°C oven. [3] Bake for about 20 minutes and check the level of the liquid and the doneness of the carrots by poking through them with a paring knife. Once you can penetrate them, without effort, they are done. If the liquid has evaporated before the carrots are done, add more liquid; if they're still swimming in liquid as they start to soften, turn the oven up to 500°F/260°C. If they're approaching doneness, remove the foil or parchment so the liquid evaporates more quickly.

Continued >>

When to Cover, When Not

What is the logic behind covering a pan or pot? Most of the time, we cover a pan or pot when we're heating liquid. The lid holds in heat—the higher the temperature, the greater the effect—until the liquid comes to a boil. We cover when we braise and stew, and we cook uncovered when poaching or boiling. Braising with the cover off causes aromatic compounds to evaporate and leaves a stew tasting flat. Cooking green vegetables with the cover on can turn them gray.

What about directions that call for partial covering? The purpose of partial covering is to allow liquid contained in the pan or pot to boil down and concentrate while still retaining the heat. The heat contained in the pan or pot is essential for cooking foods that protrude above the surface of a braising liquid. Partial covering is an alternative to directions that call for covering with a sheet of parchment paper or aluminum foil.

To glaze carrot wedges, you may want to take out the woody core first. **[1]** Cut the carrots into sections. **[2]** Cut each of the sections into wedges. The number of wedges you get out of each carrot will depend on the size of the section. In other words, you might get as many as five wedges from a section from the thick end of the carrot and as few as two from the thin end. **[3]** While it's perfectly fine to use these sections as they are, if you want to remove the core, insert a paring knife along one side of the core and snap it out. Once the carrots are cored, you may want to trim the edges a little to round them off, but this is just for looks. **[4]** Spread the carrot wedges in a heavy-bottomed pan in a single layer and add a pat of butter. Ideally there should be just enough carrots to cover the bottom of the pan. **[5]** Cover the pan with a sheet of parchment paper or aluminum foil, or partially cover it with a lid. Heat over high heat until the liquid comes to the boil and then turn down the heat to keep it at a bare simmer. Now this is the trick: You want the water (or broth) to evaporate just as the carrots are done. **[6]** To achieve this, check them from time to time by piercing them with a paring knife. If they are still hard and most of the glazing liquid has evaporated, add a little more liquid. If they're beginning to soften and there's still plenty of liquid in the pan, turn up the heat and remove the parchment paper or aluminum foil to evaporate the liquid quickly.

Fried Potatoes

Fried potatoes include potato chips, soufflé potatoes, and three kinds of french fries: very thin straw potatoes, semithin matchstick potatoes (the typical shoestring french fry), and thick steak fries. The trick to success for these fried potatoes is to control the cooking temperature. If the cooking oil is too hot, the potatoes will brown but be raw inside. If the temperature is too low, the potatoes will be soggy and oily. In the case of matchstick and steak fries, the potatoes must be fried twice—an initial poaching followed by frying in hotter oil to brown the fries and give a crispy outer coating. The most reliable method for determining doneness is to bite into a piece. French fries you're frying twice should be easily crushed between two fingers after the first frying.

Russets, preferably those that have aged a while, are the best potatoes for frying. Nowadays, most people fry potatoes in vegetable oil, but not so many years ago, before our obsession with such things as cholesterol, we fried in animal fat. Animal fats are great for frying because of their high smoking point and, most of all, because of the flavor they impart. The best fat for frying is the rendered fat—called suet—from the brittle white fat that surrounds a steer's kidneys. There was a day that the corner butcher sold suet, but now if you want the genuine article, you'll need to order beef

kidney fat and render it yourself. **[1]** This is a straightforward process of cutting up the fat into manageable pieces and slowly rendering it over low to medium heat. **[2]** The fat will be clear and golden when completely rendered and strained. Cracklings, crunchy pieces of fat, will be left behind in the strainer.

STRAW POTATOES: Heat the oil or fat, at least 6 in/15 cm deep, to 360°F/180°C in a heavy-bottomed pot. Slice the potatoes on a mandoline (a metal slicer) or slice them by hand so they're ⅛ in/3 mm thick. Slice the potato crosswise (not lengthwise) so the sliced potatoes are relatively short. Rinse the potatoes in cold water, thoroughly pat them dry, and plunge them—a bit at a time and following the usual precautions— in the hot oil or fat. Fry for about 1 minute, until golden brown. If they brown before a minute is up, turn down the heat. A straw potato should be crunchy when you bite into it, with no rawness on the inside.

MATCHSTICK POTATOES: Heat the oil or fat, at least 6 in/15 cm deep, to 340°F/170°C in a heavy-bottomed pot. **[3]** It is hot enough when a potato strip floats to the surface after about 5 seconds. Slice the potatoes lengthwise on a mandoline into ¼-in-/6-mm-thick strips. Rinse in cold water and thoroughly pat dry. **[4]** Add them to the hot oil or fat in increments. **[5]** Fry for about 5 minutes, until one is soft when you crush it in your fingers. If the potatoes brown before they have cooked through, reduce the heat. If, conversely, they take longer than 5 minutes to soften, increase the heat. When all the potatoes have been cooked to this first stage they are ready for the final frying. Increase the heat until the oil reaches 370°F/185°C. **[6]** Add the once-fried potatoes in small handfuls (if you add too many at once the oil may overflow) and fry them again for about 1 minute, until pale golden brown.

STEAK FRIES: Follow the same procedure as for matchstick potatoes except cut the potatoes into ½-in-/12-mm-thick strips. Fry in 340°F/170°C oil for about 7 minutes, until easily crushed. Fry a second time, as for matchstick potatoes.

Continued >>

[7] FOR ALL FRIES: When done, remove the potatoes from the oil with a spider or skimmer and drain on paper towels before transferring to a plate to serve. Notice that the different sizes of fries take on varying degrees of color when done.

POTATO CHIPS: Freshly made potato chips are a revelation for those who already like them out of a bag. The oil must be at just the right temperature—around 370°F/185°C—so that the chips brown and turn crispy. If they are brown but not crisp, the oil temperature is too hot. If they are crisp but not brown, the oil temperature is too low. Unless you are exceptionally skilled with a knife, use a mandoline to slice the potatoes. They should be about the thickness of a dime. After slicing, put them in a bowl of cold water to prevent them from turning color (oxidizing). When ready to fry, drain and pat dry with kitchen towels (paper towels stick and tear). To make waffle potatoes, slice the potatoes on a mandoline, using the corrugated metal blade, giving the potato a 90-degree turn after each slice. **[8]** The finished chips will have a satisfying crunch and medium-brown color.

Sautéed Potatoes

There are two approaches to sautéing potatoes. The most reliable method, but not necessarily the easiest, is to pre-roast or boil the potatoes, peel if desired, slice rather thickly, and sauté over medium heat, turning gently so as not to break them, once browned on one side. The other approach is to sauté the potatoes raw. While this is the most straightforward method, it is also the trickiest because if at any point the thin crispy membrane covering the slices is compromised by getting accidentally broken with a spatula or tongs, starch will release and you'll end up with hash browns.

When sautéing raw potatoes, you're best off using clarified butter (see page 26) because if you overheat it a little it won't burn. You can also use whole butter but you'll have to constantly regulate the heat to keep the butter hot while not allowing it to burn.

[1] Heat butter over medium to high heat and arrange the potatoes in a single layer. [2] As the potatoes brown, either toss the pan to flip them or turn them over very gently with tongs. [3] As the potatoes brown on both sides, transfer them to paper towels to absorb excess fat. [4] Serve the sautéed potatoes as soon as they come out of the pan and are still crispy.

Steamed Potatoes

Small potatoes, especially fingerling potatoes (which are vaguely finger-shaped), are best for steaming. They are creamy and smooth and pretty to look at. They're great plain or with just a pat of butter.

[1] You can use a bamboo steamer or a basket-style steamer set in a stockpot. [2] There's no special secret trick to steaming—just bring the water or other liquid to a boil—but you should keep in mind that the potatoes will dry out and may even burst out of their skins, as shown here, if overcooked. For this reason, it's a good idea to start poking the potatoes after 15 minutes of cooking. Turn off the heat as soon as the potatoes are easily penetrated with a skewer.

Roasted Potatoes

Traditionally, roasted potatoes, sometimes called château potatoes, are made with turned potatoes (see "Turned Vegetables," page 68), but it's also possible to use small fingerling potatoes, peeled or not. The principle is simple. **[1]** The potatoes are browned on the stovetop over high heat with oil. **[2]** Then they are finished on the stovetop or in the oven at 400°F/200°C with butter. **[3]** They are done when easily pierced with a skewer and a crispy shell forms, protecting a morsel of purée in the center, usually after about 15 minutes.

Turned Vegetables

Some vegetables are large and need to be cut into manageable sizes. Usually this results in pieces of vegetables with straight sides. Unfortunately, when vegetables have straight sides they don't cook evenly because they don't roll around in the pan when you shake it. When vegetables are shaped and their edges rounded off, they're said to be *turned*. While some people find turned vegetables old-fashioned, there's nothing quite as dramatic as a roast surrounded with vegetables that have been carefully rounded off. The method does take some practice, but it's one of those things you can do while watching television or talking on the phone.

[1] Cut the vegetable into sections as close in size and shape as possible. Asssuming you are right-handed, hold the vegetable in your left hand and the knife in the right. [2] Place the thumb of your right hand against the base of the vegetable to give you a point of leverage. Slowly rotate the vegetable against the knife, peeling away a thin section of the vegetable as you go. The trick is to move the vegetable against the blade of the knife while hardly moving the knife. Ideally, you should trim the edges in one motion so you don't leave jagged edges. [3] Follow the shape of the vegetable, rounding off the edges in a gentle arc to produce gently rounded ovals.

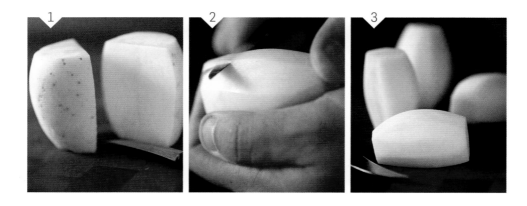

Roasted Beets

With the growing popularity of root vegetables, people are eating beets again, but many don't know how to cook them to toothsome-tender. If you're making more than a couple of beets, preheat the oven to 500°F/260°C. (If you're just cooking a beet or two, you might want to use the microwave, but remember that the microwave becomes less efficient as you put more in it. Microwave the beet for about 1 minute, turn it over, and cook for another minute, continuing in this way until it's easily pierced with a skewer.)

[1] To roast in the oven, wrap the beets in foil to keep them from making a mess. Check the beets by sliding a skewer into one. If the skewer slides in with just a little resistance, the beets are done. [2] The beets will have shrunk a bit and will be tender, but not soft, when cooked. [3] Peel the beets in a clean kitchen towel while they are still hot, rubbing them with the towel to remove the skins.

Roasted Peppers

Most peppers, unless they're thin and fragile, can be peeled by first blackening the thin outer skin. Getting the thin, transparent peel off peppers is a straightforward operation. Ideally, the peppers should be grilled over a wood fire, but most of the time we're stuck "grilling" them on the stovetop. If you have a gas stove, there's nothing to this. If you have an electric stove, with coils that glow red, a little improvisation is in order. What you need is something to keep the peppers off the surface of the coils but at the same time as close to them as possible. An uncoated metal coat hanger with thick wire works well for this. Just bend down the two ends and set the hanger over the coils with the pepper set on the wire. The wire should keep the pepper about $1/16$ in/2 mm away from the heating coils.

[1] Put the peppers directly on the flame. [2] Continue repositioning them as needed until they're blackened on all sides. As the peppers blacken, you may feel more comfortable working with one at a time. [3] The pepper is ready for peeling when the skin is blackened all over. If you're grilling the peppers and they start to turn white, you're overcooking them. [4] Many cooks like to put them in a plastic bag to help steam off the peels, but this isn't really necessary; just put them in a bowl. Allow the peppers to cool. [5] When cool enough to handle, pull away the burnt peel. [6] Once peeled, the flesh will have a deeper color than when fresh. [7] The peppers can be cut into thin strips (julienned) and used in many ways.

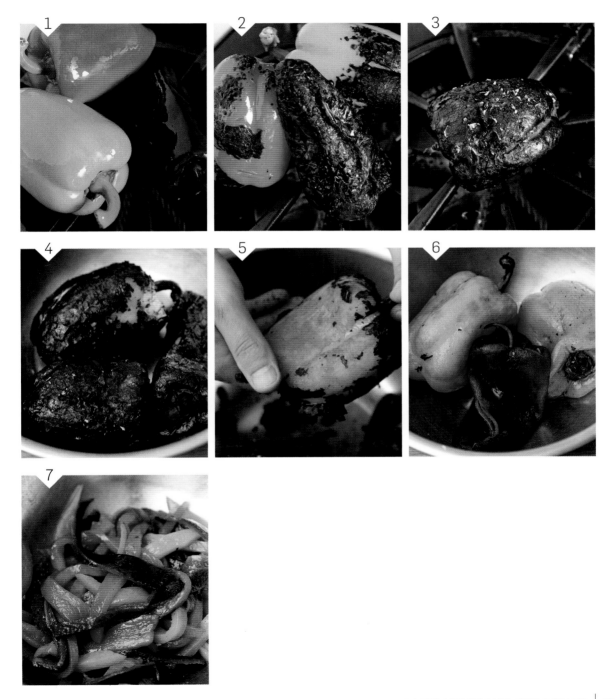

Glazed Onions

Few vegetables are as lovely or exciting as little onions that have been peeled and glazed. Small onions are not difficult to cook; it's peeling them that puts people off. If you're peeling a large number of onions—say, more than a handful—plunge them in boiling water for a minute, then drain and rinse them, to make their peels easier to remove.

The small onions that usually appear in the market are pearl onions, which are in fact the size of large pearls, and boiling onions, which are about the size of a walnut. The two are cooked in the same way.

Once you get the onions peeled, they should be glazed (see page 15). When glazing onions, there are two approaches: white glazing and brown glazing. White glazing leaves the onions coated with a transparent shiny glaze; brown glazing leaves a similar glaze except that it's a deep brown. Both approaches start the same way. [1] The onions are put in a sauté pan just large enough to hold them in a single layer. [2] Enough water or broth is added to come about one-third up the sides of the onions, the onions are covered loosely with parchment paper or aluminum foil, and simmered over medium heat. The pan should be moved rapidly back and forth every few minutes to redistribute the onions and get them to cook evenly. As the onions approach doneness, the water or broth should be just about completely evaporated so it forms a glaze that coats the onions. [3] When all the liquid has evaporated and the onions are easily penetrated with the tip of a paring knife, they're done.

When brown glazing, there's an extra step. When the liquid has evaporated, keep gently moving the pan back and forth over medium heat until the glaze browns on the bottom of the pan. Add about ¼ cup/60 ml of liquid—broth or water—to the pan and simmer. This second addition of liquid dissolves that part of the glaze that has browned and adhered to the bottom of the pan so that the glaze ends up brown. Cook down to a glaze. If you want the onions browner, repeat the process. [4] Once you've glazed your onions—either method is fine—it's easy to cream them. Simply add just enough cream to coat the bottom of the pan. Simmer gently until the cream coats the onions.

Sautéed Mushrooms

Most mushrooms contain a lot of water, which they release into the pan as soon as they get hot. Once released into a sauté pan, this water starts a chain reaction in which all the mushrooms end up steaming and eventually boiling in their own juices.

While this doesn't happen with all mushrooms—chanterelles and morels are pretty dry—it's best always to be cautious and start by cooking the mushrooms only a few at a time in a very hot pan. As soon as these mushrooms start to brown (indicating that most of their water has been driven out), add more mushrooms. Continue in this way until the pan is covered with a single layer of mushrooms.

Sautéing in butter is somewhat problematic because it isn't possible to get the pan hot enough without burning the butter. [1] To manage it, heat about 3 tablespoons butter in a large sauté pan (use as large a pan as you need to hold the mushrooms in a single layer). Control the heat so the butter barely froths—if it starts to brown, turn down the heat—and add mushrooms a few at a time. [2] Continue to sauté until the mushrooms brown and shrivel. [3] Keep adding mushrooms as each batch browns.

If you're using oil or animal fat such as duck fat or goose fat, you'll have an easier time getting the pan hot enough for the mushrooms without burning the fat because oil and animal fat can be heated to the requisite high temperature.

[4] Mushrooms are done when they are well browned, indicating that all the water they contained has been boiled down and concentrated within the mushroom.

Blanched Spinach

Other than the monotony of stemming and cleaning, spinach requires little skill in the kitchen and no special tricks for determining doneness. The spinach is done as soon as the leaves turn limp, which is usually immediately. There is no need to cook spinach beyond this stage, although you may then continue cooking it using a different cooking method—as in creamed spinach. When blanching spinach, be sure to use a lot of well-salted water (don't worry, the salt washes off and keeps the spinach green) so that the water doesn't cool off and cause the spinach to stew.

[1] Put the cleaned spinach in a large pot of well-salted boiling water. [2] The spinach is ready when it wilts, after a few seconds. [3] Drain and rinse the spinach. The leaves will be bright green and retain some of their leaflike structure. Serve immediately.

Simmered Artichokes

An artichoke is a simple thing to cook—it's just boiled in water—but knowing when it's done can be a little tricky. The best test is to slide a metal skewer into the base of the artichoke right next to the stem and judge the resistance. It should definitely resist, but not too much, a little bit like a baked potato. Another test is to pull off a leaf or two from the base and see if the flesh comes off when you scrape it between your front teeth. Third, I find that artichokes are just about right as soon as they start smelling up the kitchen.

The least onerous method of approaching an artichoke is simply to boil it, but recipes—especially French classic ones—using just the artichoke heart abound. Artichoke hearts are cooked in the same way as whole artichokes—in boiling water—and are cooked to the same degree.

[1] To prepare artichoke hearts, hold a sharp knife perpendicular to the base of the artichoke and rotate the artichoke against the blade, slicing off leaves as you go. It may take several rotations to reach the white flesh. [2] Use a smaller knife to continue trimming the green that attaches to the heart. [3] Cut off and discard the leaves. [4] Trim off any remaining pieces of green from the heart. [5] The trimmed artichoke heart, with its choke, will quickly brown (oxidize) when exposed to air. [6] Simmer the artichoke hearts in boiling water. [7] Check doneness by inserting a skewer into the heart. [8] Use a spoon to scoop out the choke. [9] Cut the heart into wedges for use in a salad or other preparation.

[1] If you're cooking a whole artichoke, cut the stem off the artichoke so it stays flat on the plate. [2] Trim the fibers and any leaves off the sides of the stem. Slice the stem into rounds. [3] Put the artichoke and stem in a pot of boiling water. Put a plate in the pot to keep the artichoke below the surface. The artichoke is done when you can insert a skewer into the base. [4] Another test is to pull a leaf and scrape it between your teeth. The flesh easily pulls away from a leaf when the artichoke is cooked. [5] As you eat the artichoke and you've worked your way down to the inner, pale leaves, pull them away to reveal the heart. [6] Remove the choke with a spoon.

Continued >>

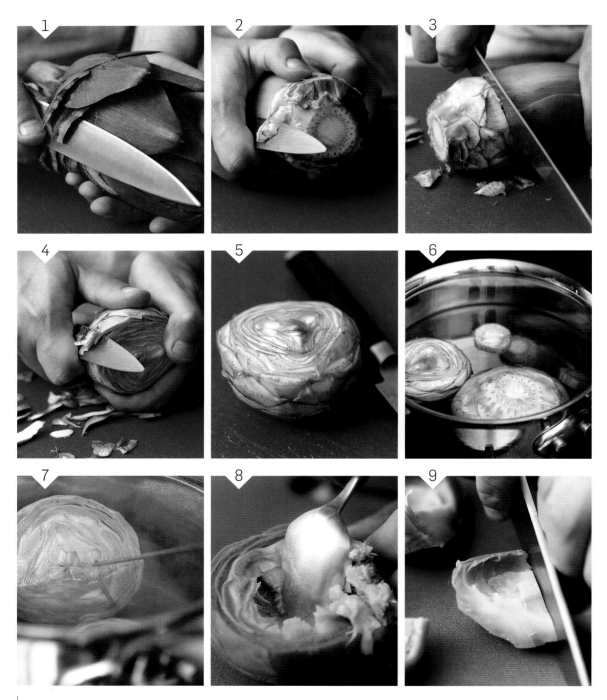

Blanched, Roasted, or Sautéed Brussels Sprouts

Most of us encounter Brussels sprouts in little boxes covered with cellophane, but if you go to a farmers' market in the fall, you're likely to encounter Brussels sprouts on the hoof, so to speak. They come attached to stalks that look somewhat like vegetable DNA.

[1] Preparing the sprouts for cooking is a simple matter of cutting them off the stalk. There are several ways to approach cooking Brussels sprouts. They can be simply boiled and finished with a little butter after draining. They can be coated with a little olive oil and roasted at 400°F/200°C; roasting concentrates their flavor and caramelizes them. Brussels sprouts can also be sautéed, with or without a preliminary blanching in boiling water.

The secret to Brussels sprouts is adding some kind of smoky element, preferably one derived from pork. Bacon is the most obvious, but other smoked meats will work as well. To use bacon, simply render it and use the fat to cook the Brussels sprouts in a frying pan. Add the bacon bits to the Brussels sprouts just before serving.

When properly cooked, Brussels sprouts should retain some texture and even a hint of crunch. To find out if the Brussels sprouts are done, pierce one with a knife or skewer, which should be able to go through, but with some resistance. (Of course, you may also want to just bite into one to test it.)

[2] To make sautéed Brussels sprouts, first quarter them and blanch them in boiling salted water. Don't cook the sprouts until soft at this stage—they should remain crunchy. [3] Drain the sprouts or take them out with a spider or skimmer.

[4] Sauté the blanched Brussels sprouts in olive oil or bacon fat. [5] Continue to sauté until the sprouts brown and caramelize and soften slightly. The finished Brussels sprouts should be lightly browned and smell fragrant. [6] They should offer resistance when poked with a skewer but not so much that they'll be difficult to chew.

Boiled, Steamed, or Roasted Asparagus

Recipe books abound with methods for cooking asparagus, which can be boiled, steamed, or roasted. Some insist that the asparagus be tied up with string and submerged in increments in boiling water so it cooks evenly. [1] The best and simplest method is to cut off and discard about 1 in/2.5 cm of the stems at the base. [2] Next, peel the asparagus stems so they cook at the same time as the flowers at the tips. By removing the tough outer fibers from each spear, it's possible to eat the entire asparagus.

To boil asparagus, simply cook the stalks in a pot of boiling water, transferring them to a colander to drain as soon as you can slide a knife blade through the biggest stalk and feel slight resistance.

To steam asparagus, use a steamer such as a basket-style or bamboo steamer.

To roast, simply coat the asparagus with olive oil and cook until brown in a 400°F/200°C oven.

While it used to be that people tended to overcook vegetables, nowadays we see the opposite trend. A properly cooked asparagus spear should offer just the slightest resistance to the tooth, but it should not be crunchy. [3] When asparagus is undercooked, it sticks straight out when you hold a spear sideways. [4] When properly cooked, it droops when you hold a spear sideways. [5] Cooked (green) asparagus will be bright green.

Braised Fennel

Fennel is a terribly underrated vegetable. It's versatile and inexpensive and can easily be converted into a cold salad or a hot accompaniment. Braising is the cooking method of choice. [1] To accomplish this, cut the fennel into wedges. Be sure to leave a little of the central core attached to the wedges to hold them together. Arrange the wedges in a pan just large enough to hold them in a single layer. Add enough broth, water, or cream to come about one-third up their sides. [2] Cover the wedges with a round of aluminum foil. [3] Simmer over low to medium heat (or put in a low- to medium-temperature oven) until the fennel is easily pierced with a paring knife.

Steamed Broccoli

Cooking broccoli is pretty straightforward. Just keep in mind that it overcooks in seconds.

[1] When you're ready to cook your broccoli, trim the florets off the large thick stems. **[2]** Put the broccoli in the steamer. **[3]** Steam the broccoli for approximately 3 minutes, or until it is bright green and the stems offer some resistance when pierced with a skewer and the florets offer almost no resistance at all.

Blanched Green Beans

While green beans are easy to prepare—just toss them in a pot of boiling salted water or steam them—there is a lot of disagreement as to how much they should be cooked. In the old days, green beans were boiled until completely soft and were then typically finished with butter. Nowadays we like our string beans with some crunch, but almost everyone undercooks them, leaving them raw tasting and too toothsome. Ideally, they should have just a trace of crunch, usually accomplished by 4 to 5 minutes of cooking.

Again, like so many foods, the best way to determine doneness—especially since it's largely a matter of taste—is to just bite into one and determine if it has the right amount of crunch. Once you get used to cooking green beans, you'll be able to determine their doneness by how they feel in the pan when you stir them.

[1] To cook the green beans, boil them in plenty of salted water. (The salt is important for preserving the color, but washes off the beans.) [2] Once the water comes back to a boil and the beans turn bright green, snap open a bean; a crisp snap indicates the bean is cooked but still crunchy and is done cooking. As the beans cook further, they will no longer snap (they will bend). If you're serving the hot green beans right away, pour them into a colander to drain, then toss them with a pat of cold butter. (Don't make the common mistake of heating the green beans with butter, which will turn the butter oily.) [3] If you are not serving the beans immediately, remove them from the boiling water with a spider skimmer. [4] Transfer the beans to a bowl of cold water to stop the cooking. As soon as they've completely cooled, drain the green beans.

Steamed or Sautéed Zucchini

I've always found zucchini to be rather anemic and tasteless unless cooked properly. There are two approaches: steaming and sautéing. When steaming, cut the slices rather thick—about ¼ in/6 mm—and steam them for just a minute or two, until they turn a brighter green. Don't try steaming too many pieces at once—keep them in a single layer in the steamer—or you'll end up with a soggy mess. Season with salt and pepper and serve.

Steaming is best when you want to retain the zucchini's delicate flavor. When you want the flavor to be more robust, you're best off sautéing. Sautéing is an excellent method because zucchini contain a lot of water that has to be driven off to concentrate the flavor.

Most people sauté with too much zucchini in the pan at the beginning. This, of course, generates steam, which turns the zucchini into mush. [1] To sauté properly, heat a few tablespoons of olive oil in the largest sauté pan you have until the oil ripples. Add enough zucchini slices (in this case they should be about ⅛ in/3 mm thick) to create a single layer. [2] Sauté over high heat until the slices wither and barely begin to brown. Add another handful of slices, continue to sauté, and continue in this way until you've added all the zucchini. [3] Sauté until the slices lose their moisture and turn golden brown.

Zucchini are delicious finished with garlic and parsley butter. They are also good with fresh chopped marjoram.

Rice Pilaf

To make a simple version of rice pilaf, gently cook (sweat) a chopped onion in a sauté pan, add the rice, and cook for a few minutes to lightly toast the rice. Add twice the volume of water to rice to the pan. Stir and then cover the pan with parchment paper and a lid. Cook the rice over low to medium heat on the stove or in a 325°F/165°C oven.

[1] When the rice pilaf has been cooking for about 15 minutes, notice how small the grains are and how dull they are rather than being bright white. They are only partially cooked. [2] When the pilaf is done, the grains are white, opaque, and swollen, indicating that the pilaf is cooked. If the rice bursts open, you've overcooked it.
[3] Take two forks and dig into the rice while lifting to fluff up the grains before serving.

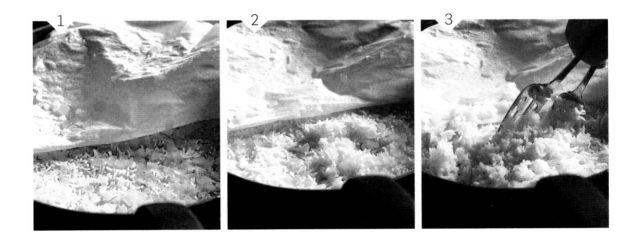

Risotto

A well-executed risotto should consist of perfectly cooked grains of rice held together by a savory sauce derived from the rice itself. There is much debate over how runny or thick risotto should be, with people in Venice preferring it almost souplike and other regions of Italy liking it rather stiff. But this is entirely up to you and is a simple matter of adding more or less liquid to the risotto at the end of the cooking process. More important is the texture of the individual grains of rice. The idea is for the rice to be thoroughly cooked yet retain a slight resistance to the tooth. If the risotto turns mushy, you've overcooked it.

The only way to check if your risotto is done is to bite into a rice grain. Once the grains have the right texture, serve the risotto immediately so it doesn't overcook.

Risotto puts people off because they think they have to spend a long 20 minutes at the stove stirring rice. While this is true, it's not necessary to do it all at once. In other words, earlier in the day, you can cook the risotto for about 10 minutes and then cover it (once it cools) with plastic wrap pressed against its surface. If you're not serving it within a couple of hours, refrigerate the risotto. When you're ready to serve, resume cooking and the risotto will be done in about 10 minutes.

Risotto requires short-grain rice such as Carnaroli or Arborio. Italians are insistent on using one variety over the other, depending on what region they're from. In my own experience, they function much the same.

Few risottos are as simple (or as good) as the classic *risotto alla milanese*, made by gently sautéing (sweating) an onion, adding chicken broth, flavoring with saffron, and topping with freshly grated Parmigiano-Reggiano.

[1] Soak a pinch of saffron in a teaspoon or so of water in a bowl. [2] In a sauce-pan, gently cook (sweat) a finely chopped onion in butter. Stir in the rice. Cook over gentle heat for about 5 minutes, until the rice grains turn opaque. [3] Pour in broth, 1 cup/240 ml at a time, and continue stirring over medium heat. [4] Continue stirring and adding broth as the rice absorbs the liquid. [5] Notice how the underdone grains are small, compact, and have opaque centers. [6] Cooked grains will have expanded and turned slightly translucent. [7] Finished risotto will appear moist around the edges and the grains will retain their distinct shape. Grate Parmigiano-Reggiano over and serve.

Cooked Dried Beans

Most recipes say to soak dried beans. While soaking does cut the cooking time by about 30 minutes, it is by no means essential.

Most of us are discouraged from preparing beans because of their long cooking times. (Some beans from India take up to 5 hours to cook!) This is where the pressure cooker comes in handy. Beans that might normally take 2 hours to cook are done in 20 to 30 minutes, depending on the how much pressure your pressure cooker delivers.

Because pressure cookers are not standardized (mine has two settings for pressure levels), you'll have to keep opening up your cooker to check the beans until you figure out how long they take. In the future, you can simply time the beans to know when they're done.

[1] If you have time, begin by soaking beans in enough water so that as they expand they don't protrude from the surface of the water. [2] After soaking for several hours or overnight the beans will have expanded. [3] If you're using a pressure cooker, put the beans in the pot with enough water to cover by about 1 in/2.5 cm. The time will depend on your pressure cooker, but start checking the beans after 30 minutes. If you're not using a pressure cooker, simply cook the beans, uncovered, in enough water to cover until they soften, which can take 1 to 5 hours, depending on the type of bean. Beans are done when you can easily crush them between two fingers. [4] Beans should not burst out of their skins, as shown here, which indicates they've been overcooked.

SEA
FOOD

Poached Oysters

One of the easiest ways to serve cooked oysters is simply to poach them in their own liquid, scoop them out with a slotted spoon, add a little cream to the poaching liquid, boil it down slightly, put the oysters back in, and serve. This, I suspect, is the technique for the famous oyster panfry at the Grand Central Oyster Bar, in New York.

Many people dislike cooked oysters. I can't possibly imagine hating cooked oysters, unless the oysters have been overcooked and turned into little mucosal blobs. When poaching an oyster, never allow the liquid to come to full boil. [1] The oysters will appear near-translucent before they've been heated. [2] As you poach them, they should just froth up a bit and firm up so that instead of looking amorphous, they separate from one another. If you continue to cook the oysters, they will lose volume and harden.

Steamed Mussels and Clams

Steam mussels and clams in a pot with liquid such as water, wine, cider, or fish broth. Cover the pot, bring the liquid to full boil, and steam the clams or mussels until they open. To say *steaming* is somewhat inaccurate, because much of the time the mussels or clams are in contact or even partially submerged in the liquid. Fortunately, this seems to have little effect on how they cook.

Yes, it is true that clams and mussels should be tightly closed when you buy them. This is assuredly true for clams, but mussels often gape a bit if they're left undisturbed. If a mussel is gaping, tap it on a hard surface and see if this causes it to close slightly. Sometimes it may take 5 minutes or so for it to close, so be patient.

[1] The steaming liquid for mussels can be simmered with garlic, shallots, tomatoes, parsley, or red pepper flakes to infuse the flavors before you use it to cook the mussels. [2] Put the mussels in a pot with the steaming liquid and cover tightly. [3] As you steam the mussels, you'll see that they open almost immediately. [4] You can see how the meat clings to both shells. If you take the mussels out of the pot too soon, the meat will tear when you try to extract it. [5] When the mussels are fully cooked, usually within 5 minutes, the meat pulls away from one shell. If you find a mussel or two that didn't open, carefully remove them—they often are full of mud—and throw them out.

[6] Clams can be steamed with the same liquids as mussels. I typically use a mixture of white wine, parsley, and chopped tomatoes. [7] Clams pop open all at once, usually within 10 minutes, so you don't have to worry about their meat clinging to both shells. Clams will sometimes refuse to open even when perfectly good. If you have clams that won't open, stick a knife in the slit between the two shells and give it a twist. The shells should pop open. If the shells separate with no resistance, it means the clam is dead and you should just throw it out.

Continued >>

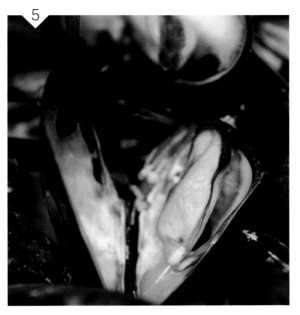

Steamed or Sautéed Scallops

Most of us have never seen a scallop in the shell, the iconic seashell of Shell Oil Company. But when it is possible to find scallops in the shell, grab the chance because it may be your only opportunity to find a scallop that is alive and, hence, perfectly fresh.

Most scallops are harvested on ships that stay out to sea for as long as 2 weeks, flash-freezing most of their catch. [1] When you shuck a scallop out of the shell, you're guaranteed a truly fresh scallop—in fact, one that was alive until you shucked it. [2] To open a scallop, slide a knife into the opening between the two shells. Slide it along the underside of the bottom shell, detaching the scallop as you go. Be very careful at this stage to avoid cutting into the scallop. [3] Slide a knife under the top shell to detach the scallop and the surrounding innards. [4] Pull the innards and membrane away from the scallop.

[5] Among these innards is the roe, which wraps around the scallop like a little tongue. Much of the time the roe is an ugly gray and is best thrown out; but when it's an appealing red or pink, go ahead and cook the roe along with the scallop, or purée it by working it through a strainer and use it to make a tasty sauce.

Escoffier's *Le Guide Culinaire* gives a recipe for scallops that involves blanching them for 20 minutes, putting them back in their shells on a bed of cooked chopped mushrooms (called *duxelles*), covering them with béchamel sauce, and then sliding them under the broiler. This is a great option if you can't stand the taste and texture of fresh scallops.

[6] My approach is the opposite and, at the risk of being controversial, I think that the absolute best way to eat scallops this fresh is raw, with perhaps a few drops of lemon juice, nothing more. If you do insist on cooking the scallops, they are best steamed or sautéed. When sautéed, use high heat to guarantee the formation of a savory crust before the scallop has a chance to cook through. Here, again, even when cooked, the inside of a scallop should remain essentially raw, but at least warm.

[7] To sauté the scallops, use a small, sharp knife to make shallow score marks on each scallop. This is primarily decorative and completely optional. Heat oil until smoking hot in a small saucepan and sauté for approximately 1 minute on each side. [8] When the scallop is perfectly cooked it is still translucent inside but not cold. [9] The dish shown here was made by puréeing the roe and working the purée into a small amount of beurre blanc, a rich butter sauce based on vinegar, wine, and shallots.

Shrimp Tempura

There are a couple of little tricks for successful tempura. First, the batter should be worked as little as possible. While it may be counterintuitive, a good tempura batter should contain lumps and be barely stirred. When frying shrimp tempura, the temperature of the oil should be as hot as possible so the tempura batter becomes crispy before the food has time to overcook. Recipes often instruct to fry shrimp for 2 minutes, which only results in dried-out shrimp. Ideally, the shrimp should be fried in extremely hot oil (heated until the oil just starts to smoke), in which it will cook in about 5 seconds. It can be difficult to balance cooking the tempura batter and the shrimp perfectly.

The best way to make tempura at home is this technique: Heat 4 to 6 in/10 to 15 cm of vegetable oil in a heavy-bottomed pot. [1] Stir together 2 to 4 egg yolks (depending on how many shrimp you are battering), a few tablespoons of water, and enough cake flour (cake flour is used because of its low gluten content) to make a batter. [2] Stir with chopsticks as little as possible, stirring just enough to blend but not to completely mix in the lumps. [3] Coat the shrimp with cake flour. [4] Dip the shrimp in the batter. Bring the oil to about 390°F/195°C, but lower the heat if it begins smoking at any time. [5] Drop in the battered shrimp six to ten at a time and fry just until the batter is golden brown—no longer, or the shrimp will be overcooked. [6] Using a spider or skimmer, transfer them to a plate lined with paper towels to drain. Check the heat of the oil, waiting for it to return to 390°F/195°C or hotter before cooking more shrimp.

Boiled Lobster

Most people overcook lobster in the same way they overcook chicken.

Lobster, of course, is cooked using various methods. The one we all know best is simply to boil (or, better, poach) the lobster in hot water. Other methods require you to cut up the lobster and cook it in a sauté pan. You can also steam lobster. [1] Whichever method you use, kill the lobster humanely first by plunging a knife into its head through the top.

However you cook your lobster, it's a good trick to slide a wooden skewer through the lobster tail, along the inside of the bottom of the shell. This keeps the tail from curling during cooking.

[2] If you're boiling the lobster, it's best to rely on time rather than on any particular indicators. A 1¼-lb/570-g lobster will cook in 3 minutes. Add a minute for each additional ½ lb/225 g. [3] Of course, this runs counter to anything ever written about lobster—most sources say to cook a 2-lb/910-g lobster for 20 minutes when in fact it's done in 4 minutes, with a 2-minute rest.

There is, however, an inherent difficulty. Female lobsters contain dark green roe—which also happens to be the very tastiest part of the lobster—which turns bright orange when it gets to a certain temperature. [4] If you cook the lobster as described here, you'll find that the roe remains dark green, almost black. [5] While raw lobster roe contains the absolute essence of lobster, most people won't want to eat spoonfuls of black miniature eggs.

The best solution is to pull the roe out of the cooked lobster and turn it into a sauce. Work the roe through a fine-mesh strainer with your clean fingers into a bowl with a teaspoon of wine vinegar or Cognac in it to prevent clotting. [6] Combine the roe with several tablespoons (a couple or so per lobster) of the steaming liquid or water and whisk over medium heat until the mixture turns orange and thickens into a sauce you can spoon around the cooked lobster meat.

[7] You can also circumvent the roe problem by simply cooking the lobster for the usual recommended time—20 minutes or so—leaving the lobster tough and overcooked but the roe bright orange instead of black.

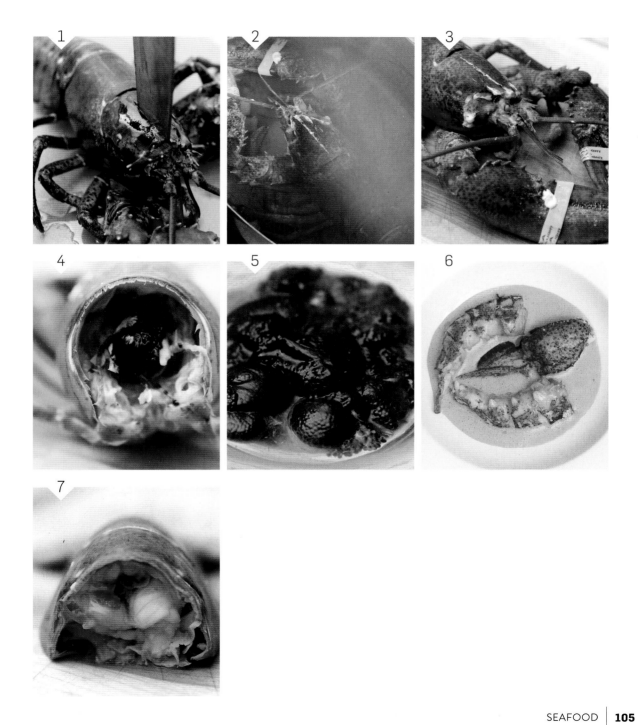

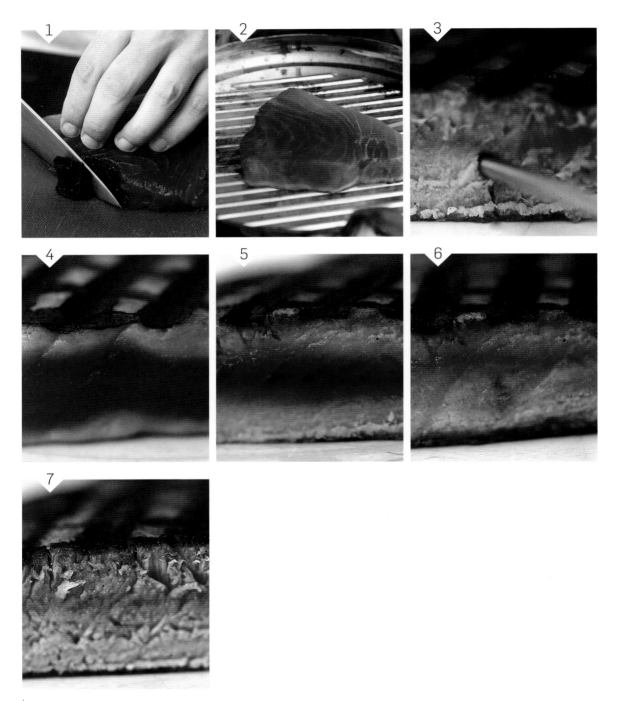

Grilled Tuna Steak

It wasn't so long ago that Americans' only contact with tuna was out of a can. Things have changed considerably since then and we enjoy fresh tuna, usually cooked rare or left almost raw on the inside, creating the effect of sashimi, but with a savory and crispy crust. If you want to cook your tuna more, you can take it to the point where it just starts to lose its red color, a tad more than medium-rare—cooking it any more than this will just dry it out.

Always allow the tuna steak to come to room temperature before cooking. Tuna can be grilled over very high heat because it releases little fat, so it doesn't cause flare-ups. Of course, the thinner the steak, the hotter your "fire," or heat source, should be and, if grilling, the closer the tuna should be to the heat. If the steak is very thick—more than 1 in/2.5 cm—build a fire to one side, brown the tuna on both sides over the fire, and then move the tuna away from the fire to the side. Cover the grill, but leave the vents open. If you don't have a covered grill, cook thick tuna steaks over a lower fire that's at least 6 in/15 cm away from the grill.

Determining doneness of a tuna steak can be a little tricky, especially because there are different degrees to which we can cook it. The best method is to stick an instant-read thermometer into the center of the steak through the side.

If you don't have a thermometer, you'll have to judge the steak by texture and juice formation. If you're cooking the steak very rare, it will simply brown and blacken on the outside. The steak should feel fleshy and release no juices. As the steak approaches a more cooked rare or medium-rare, it starts to release liquid. When cooked medium-rare, it bounces when you press the surface (as opposed to sinking in and retaining the depression you made with your finger). As soon as it bounces back to the touch, it's done.

[1] In any case, when you get your tuna, trim off any dark red or brown patches. Fire up the grill so it's very hot. [2] Grill for about 1 minute. Give the tuna a 90-degree turn, and grill for 1 minute more. This creates a professional-looking crosshatch pattern on the fish. By observing the side of the tuna steak as it cooks, you can see how the tuna cooks from rare to cooked all the way through. [3] If you're unsure how the tuna should feel at various stages of doneness, stick an instant-read thermometer in through the side. After you remove the tuna from the heat, it will continue to cook for 5 minutes or so as it rests. [4] Raw to very rare will read 115°F/45°C. [5] Rare will read 120°F/48°C. [6] Medium-rare will read 125°F/52°C. [7] Medium will read 130°F/54°C.

Braised Halibut

To make a simple and elegant version of braised halibut, put the halibut fillet (or fillet sections) in an ovenproof pan just large enough to hold the fish. [1] I like to scatter mushrooms around the fish, but these are, of course, optional. Add a little dry sherry—enough to come about one-quarter of the way up the sides of the fish. [2] Cover the pan loosely with parchment paper or aluminum foil. Put the pan on the stove over high heat. When the sherry starts to boil, slide the pan into a 350°F/175°C oven.

You can often know when fish is done by smell. As soon as you sense that savory, just-cooked fish smell, it's done. Of course, this can seem like a haphazard method that is not totally reliable, but once you get comfortable with other methods of testing for doneness, you'll learn to trust your nose. [3] A safer method is to take a knife and probe at the fish between the flakes, or the striations, in the flesh. When there is no sign of flaking—in other words, the so-called flakes hold together—the fish is properly done. [4] If the fish separates into flakes, it's actually overcooked. Despite what you read in many recipes, the flakes should stick together when you try to pry them apart with the knife. [5] The fish should be cooked enough so that it bounces back when you press the surface (as opposed to sinking in and retaining the depression you made with your finger). As soon as it bounces back to the touch, it's done.

Transfer the fish to a platter (if it's a whole large piece, you need to cut it into sections) or individual plates while you make the sauce. [6] Add cream to the braising liquid, reduce slightly to thicken (the sauce should still be souplike), and season with salt and pepper. Add parsley, and the sauce is ready to serve with the fish.

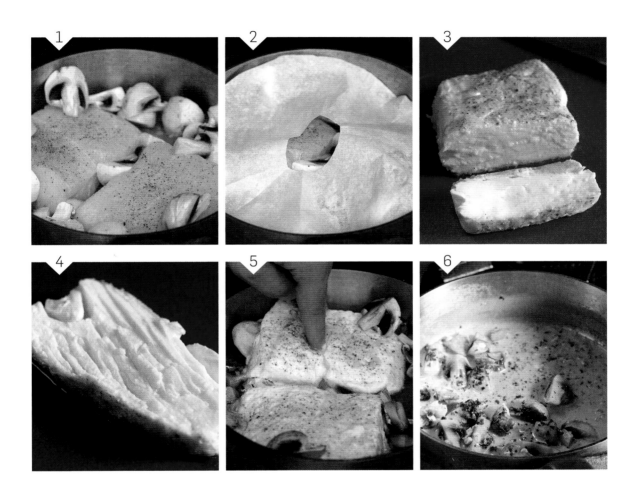

Sautéed, Grilled, or Poached Salmon Steaks and Fillets

Before you cook your salmon, be sure to remove any bones with a pair of tweezers. [1] If you're cooking steaks, you may want to cut out the central backbone and tie the steak up into a medallion. This helps the fish cook evenly and keeps the flaps from overcooking. Cut along the bone that runs between the two sides of the salmon steak. You'll feel small pinbones that connect the fillets to the backbone. Go ahead and cut through these. [2] Cut off a piece of skin from one of the flaps so that when you fold it inside the medallion you don't encounter skin. [3] Fold the flaps inward to create snug medallions.

[4] If you're poaching the salmon, poach it in vegetable broth (court bouillon) or water simmered with a bundle of fresh herbs (bouquet garni) and seasoned with salt. When the surface of the salmon looks opaque, look for the formation of white exudate and white froth, which indicates it's approaching doneness.

[5] If you're using a salmon fillet, slice it into single servings. Sauté the salmon skin-side down. Hold the salmon down with a spatula during the first few seconds of cooking to prevent the contracting skin from causing the salmon to curl. Continue sautéing on the skin side. [6] Cook for about 3 minutes to get the skin to turn crispy, then turn to cook the other side. [7] When white coagulated froth begins to form on the side of the fish fillet, it's approaching doneness.

[8] The pressure test is easy for salmon: You can tell it's done when it feels firm and bounces back when you press the surface (as opposed to sinking in and retaining the depression you made with your finger). If you haven't mastered the pressure test, stick a thermometer in through the side of the salmon and cook until the thermometer reads 130°F/54°C.

[9] Perfectly cooked salmon will be shiny and translucent in the center and opaque near the outside. [10] Overcooked salmon will appear opaque all the way through. [11] Undercooked salmon will appear raw in the center.

Continued >>

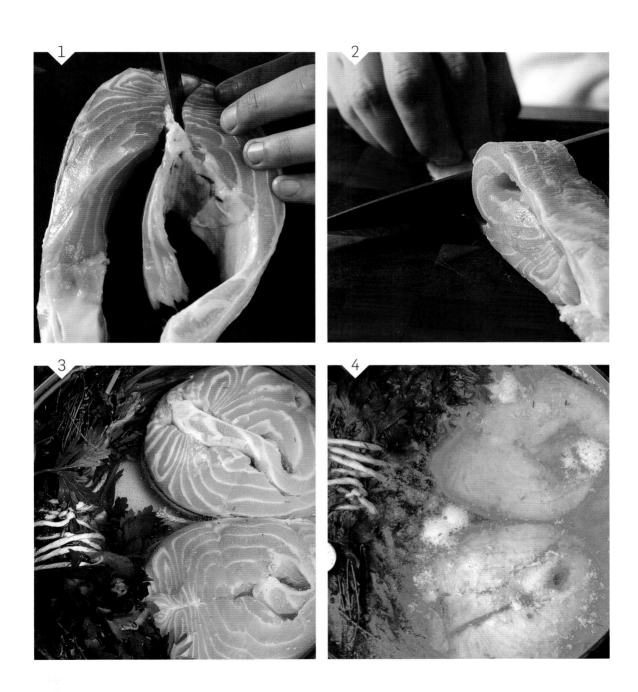

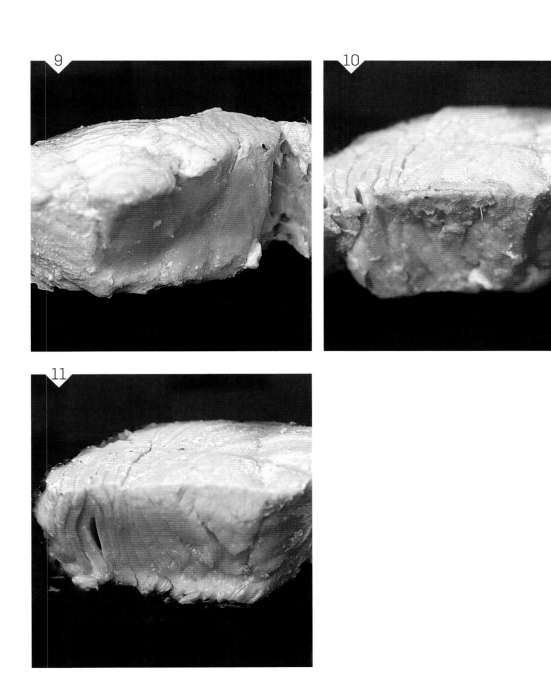

Grilled Whole Roundfish

There isn't much to grilling a whole roundfish. Ideally the gills and fins should be removed—the fins are cut off mainly so you don't poke yourself—but that's about it. The scales should be left on because they will prevent the fish from sticking to the grill. When it comes time to serve, the skin and scales can just be peeled off. During the cooking they function as a protective sheath, trapping in juices. I like to grill a whole branzino, a kind of bass from the eastern Atlantic, but I can also use red snapper or porgy. Filleting a whole cooked roundfish does take some practice, but the payoff is big flavor.

[1] Wipe a grill or grill pan with oil and heat as hot as possible. [2] Put the whole fish on the grill. [3] Grill for about 5 minutes per 1 in/2.5 cm of thickness and then turn over. [4] Grill for about 4 minutes more and insert a thermometer through the back of the fish, about 1 in/2.5 cm. It should register 130°F/54°C.

Another way to determine the doneness of a whole roundfish is to slide a small knife along the back and to one side of the spinal column. Notice if the flesh is clinging to the bone or if it pulls away. If it pulls away—ideally it should resist a little—the fish is done. You can also insert a skewer into the back of the fish—go in about 1 in/2.5 cm—and then touch it to your lip. When the skewer is distinctly warm, the fish is done.

When the fish is done, it's ready to be filleted. [5] Start by peeling off the skin and scales. [6] Gently remove the top fillets with a fish knife or spatula. [7] Lift away the bones that run along the center of the fish (this is the spinal column). [8] Transfer the fillets on the platter or cutting board to a serving plate. [9] Serve drizzled with extra-virgin olive oil.

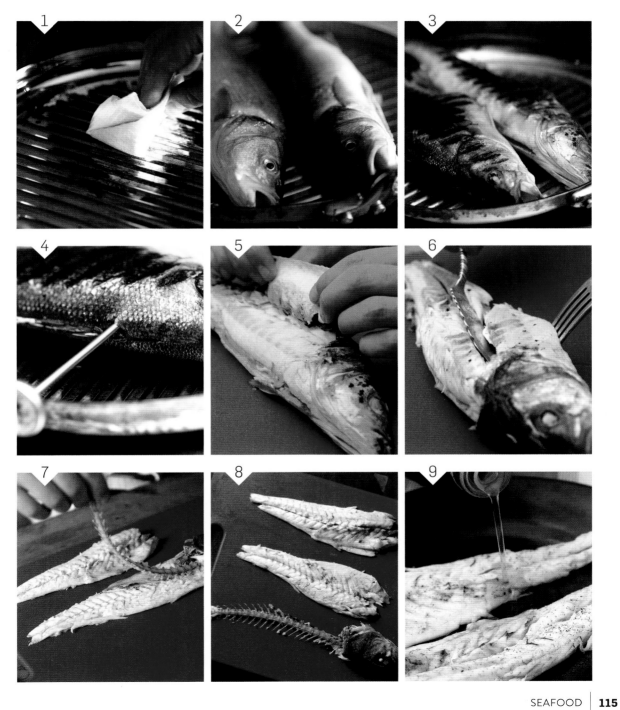

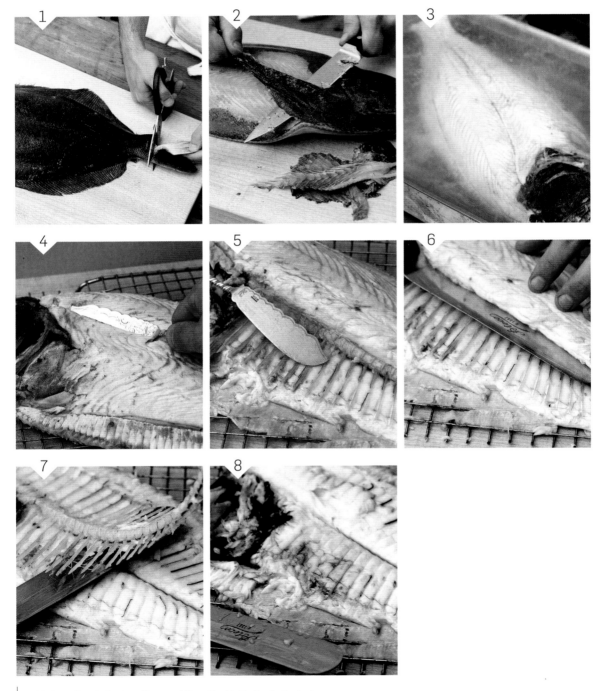

Poached Whole Flatfish

Most of us have never poached a flatfish because we're unaccustomed to eating whole fish, but as we return to previous generations' mode of "eating the whole animal," more whole fish are available and more of us are cooking them at home.

Flatfish, such as flounder, halibut, sole, turbot, and fluke, are traditionally poached in a square poacher called a *turbotière*. Such an implement seems to only be sold in copper at a price one can only imagine. Fortunately, it is possible to improvise a turbotière at home. First you need a roasting pan large and deep enough to hold the fish. Next, you need to find a wire cooling rack the same size as the roasting pan (or cut one down with wire cutters). Once you have your rack, tie string to both ends to act as handles that allow you to lift out the fish.

[1] Begin by removing the gills and the fins from the gutted fish. Scale the bottom white side of the fish by scraping it with a fish scaler or the back of a knife. It helps to do the scraping into a garbage bag to keep the scales from flying around. [2] Remove the top, black skin in strips with a knife or leave it on and peel it off after poaching.

A traditional poaching liquid would be a vegetable broth (court bouillon) but you can also make poaching liquid by tying up a large bundle of herbs (bouquet garni) and simmering it for 10 minutes in enough water to poach the fish.

Determine how much liquid you're going to need to poach the fish by putting the fish in the poacher, pouring over enough cold water to cover the fish, and then pouring out the water into a liquid measuring cup to measure it. Transfer the same amount of court bouillon to a pot, bring it to the boil, and pour it into the poacher. [3] Slide the fish into the liquid. Poach until done, about 10 minutes per 1 in/2.5 cm of thickness. [4] Doneness is determined by sliding a fish knife under one of the fillets. As you lift up the fillet it should cling to the bone but not so firmly as to be impossible to remove. If the fillet pulls away from the bone easily, the fish is probably a bit overcooked. [5] Notice the slight transparency on the bone where the fillet was removed, which indicates proper cooking. [6] Use a spatula to remove the second fillet. [7] Lift off the spinal column. [8] Gently lift off the bottom fillets and serve.

Grilled, Sautéed, or Braised Squid

While most of the time squid comes already cleaned, there may be times, especially at ethnic markets, when it comes in its natural state and needs to have its innards removed. Once cleaned, you have the hood—the hollow body—and the tentacles.

[1] To clean the squid, cut the tentacles where they join just below the eyes. [2] Pull the innards out of the hood. [3] Pull out the plasticlike quill that runs along one side of the hood. [4] Peel away the dark skin that coats the hood. This is optional, as there are those who insist the skin has a lot of flavor. [5] The hood can be cut into rings or left whole.

There are two basic ways to cook squid: cooking it very quickly by grilling or sautéing it over the highest heat possible so it has no time to toughen, or cooking it very slowly so the protein softens, usually after 30 minutes. [6] You may also combine techniques and braise the squid (red wine or tomatoes are particularly good as braising media) before grilling it to finish it just before serving.

[7] Grilled or sautéed squid are done as soon as their hoods stiffen, after about 2 minutes of cooking. To determine the doneness of squid, either bite into a piece or probe one with a skewer to get a sense of how much it resists. Grilled or sautéed squid will still be firm and even somewhat rubbery. Braised squid, which typically takes approximately 40 minutes to soften, should be perfectly tender when it is ready.

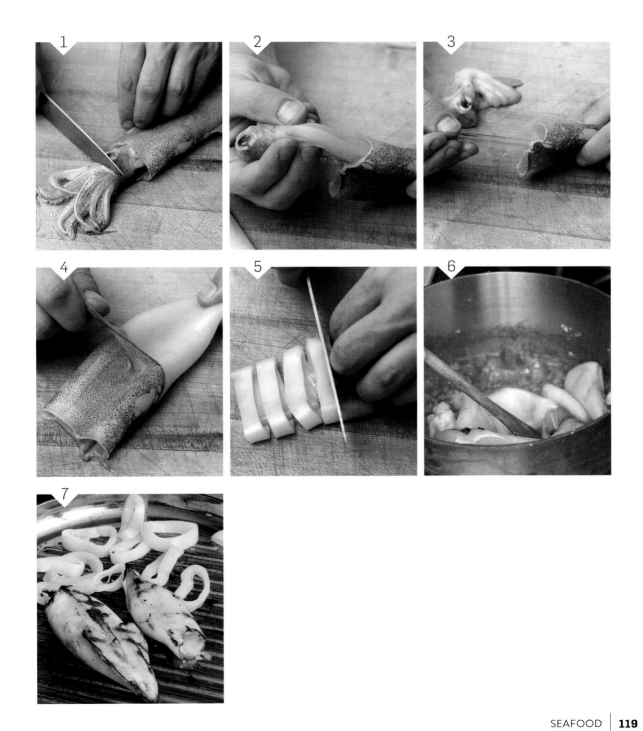

Braised or Sautéed Octopus

People tend to feel strongly about octopus and either loathe it or love it. Perhaps it isn't more popular because it tends to be rubbery and tough. There are various means of tenderizing it—such as the rustic technique of beating it against rocks, or brining it, rubbing it with shredded daikon, or marinating it with tropical vegetables—but if you braise it, you can be sure that it will be plenty tender and savory. In fact, it's a good trick to braise octopus before grilling or sautéing it to create the effect of great tenderness. This eliminates the need for any of the machinations people go through to soften it up.

Octopus usually comes cleaned (in fact, it's often frozen), but if it comes uncleaned, the process of cleaning it is easy. [1] Remove the small "beak" that's visible on one side of the head. [2] Cut away and discard the head.

[3] I recommend braising octopus in the classic way: Aromatic vegetables are gently sautéed (sweated). The octopus (I prefer to use baby octopus) is typically cut up into 1-in/2.5-cm lengths and added to the aromatic vegetables. [4] The mixture cooks until any liquid released by the octopus dries on the bottom of the pan. [5] Add wine, along with a bundle of fresh herbs (bouquet garni), and let the whole thing simmer for about 45 minutes. [6] Check for doneness by inserting a knife into the octopus, which should give only slight resistance. When the octopus is done, simply lift it out of the braising liquid. Strain the braising liquid through a fine-mesh strainer into a saucepan. Heat over medium-high heat until it is reduced and slightly thickened. Serve it spooned over the octopus.

[7] If you find baby octopus, you may also sauté it for 3 minutes on each side and serve it straightaway. It won't be as tender as if it had been braised, but it will retain its delicious sealike flavor.

POULTRY

Roast Chicken

Most people roast chickens to death. It doesn't help that most recipe books say to cook the bird until it reaches a temperature of 160°F/71°C (some even more) when the correct temperature (taken where the thighbone joins the rest of the bird) is 140°F/60°C. [1] The first trick for avoiding this is to cover the breast loosely with aluminum foil during the first 20 minutes of roasting. This slows down the cooking of the breast such that it ends up done at the same time as the thighs. Keep in mind, also, that a properly roasted chicken is going to be pink on the thigh where it meets the breast. If this bothers you and you prefer to see the thighs more "done," your best bet is to take the chicken out of the oven, carve off the thighs, and put them back in the oven for 5 minutes or so while you keep the rest of the bird warm. When the thighs are ready, carve the breasts away from the bone and serve.

Trussing the bird helps it cook evenly and also holds it together so it looks better when you serve it. [2] To truss the bird, slide a length of string under the flap of skin at the bottom end that looks like a little tail (sometimes called the "pope's nose"). [3] Cross the string over each of the drumsticks to form an X. [4] Pull the string back along the sides of the chicken's back toward its wings. [5] Flip the chicken over, hooking the string over the wings, and pull the string tight. [6] Tie tightly and your chicken is trussed.

[7] When you're ready to roast your chicken, spread a couple of chicken necks and wings (purchased in addition to the whole chicken) and a handful of aromatic vegetables over the bottom of a roasting pan. Place the whole chicken, with the breasts covered in foil, on top. [8] Roast for 20 minutes and remove the foil. The chicken thighs will be lightly browned.

Continued >>

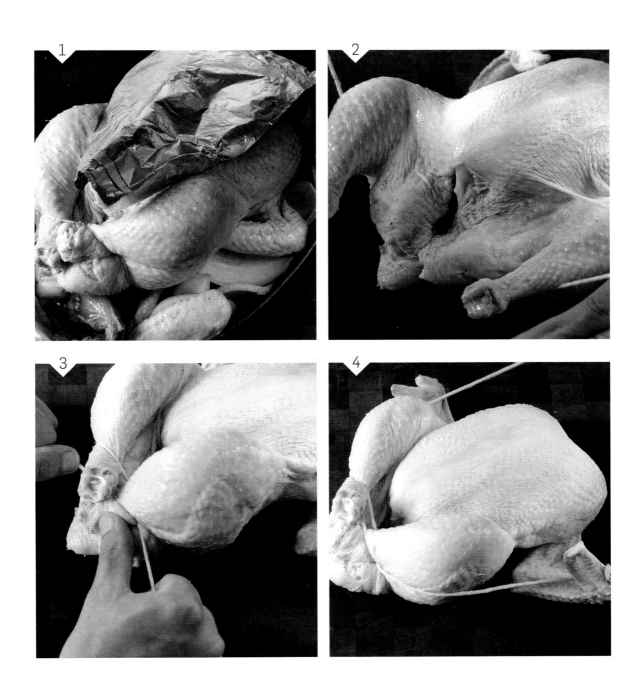

[9] The most reliable method for determining doneness is simply to use an instant-read thermometer. Poke it through the little section of skin that separates the thigh from the breast. Slide the thermometer along the inner thigh until you touch the joint—the end of the thighbone. Pull back about ¼ in/6 mm—you don't want to take a reading of the bone, which will be hotter than the meat. Leave the thermometer in for about 5 seconds. Withdraw the thermometer and immediately check the reading.

Of course, it is more challenging when you don't have a thermometer. In these situations the best method is to look at the juices that form on the inside of the bird's cavity. [10] During the first phase of roasting, they'll be cloudy and pink-red. [11] As the bird cooks, the juices become clear and streaked with dark red. This is when the bird is done. (It is not done when the juices are perfectly clear as recommended by some sources. If you wait until the juices run completely clear, your chicken meat will be overcooked and dry.)

[12] When you carve your chicken, you'll notice that it's still pink on the inside of the thigh. [13] The breast meat should be white but very moist. This is normal and is how chicken should be cooked. (Don't confuse pink with raw, however. Raw chicken will have a distinct translucency that you want to avoid.) If you find that the chicken is underdone, just stick it back in the oven for 10 minutes or so and check it again. There's no harm done in removing it from the oven to test it and then returning it to the oven to continue cooking.

Once you've roasted your chicken, you're probably going to want to make a little jus. And when I say "a little jus," the emphasis is on "little." The reason for this is that a properly roasted chicken (or any food for that matter) releases very few juices. (A chicken cooked to death will provide enough juices to make a wonderful gravy.) When you cook your chicken properly, you will find that you're left with just a couple tablespoons of liquid.

Continued >>

When you're ready to make a jus, lift up the chicken with a wooden spoon stuck in its cavity and let any juices in the cavity spill out into the roasting pan. Set the chicken on a platter, cover loosely with aluminum foil, and let rest. **[14]** Put the roasting pan, with the wings, back, and other bones, on the stove and boil down the juices until they form a brown crust on the pan and the fat is left in a clear layer on top. **[15]** Pour or scoop off the fat. **[16]** Add a splash of broth or water—about ¼ cup/60 ml per chicken—and deglaze the pan by putting it on the stove over medium-high heat and scraping it with a wooden spoon to dissolve the juices that have caramelized into a crust on the pan's surface.

Making Jus or Gravy

Jus is based on the caramelized juices that collect on the bottom of the pan while a cut of meat is roasting. Several challenges commonly arise when making jus. First, if the roast is cooked rare (such as a rib roast), it's not going to release much in the way of juices. Because of this, the juices are completely dependent on what you put in the roasting pan. If, when you take out the roast, you find that the juices are caramelized in a brown crust on the bottom of the pan, you need only remove the fat that floats on top. This can be simply poured out or removed with a spoon. Once the fat has been removed, you then deglaze the pan by adding a liquid such as water, broth, or wine. Use a minimum of liquid to deglaze the pan—about ¼ cup/60 ml (which will reduce down)—or the jus will be weak. You then place the pan on the stove and scrape the bottom with a wooden spoon. As soon as the juices dissolve, strain them and serve them in a sauceboat at the table. You should end up with about 2 tablespoons of jus per serving.

If, when you take the roast out of the oven, you find a small amount of cloudy jus in the bottom of the pan, you'll have to remove the fat that has emulsified in the juices and made them cloudy. To do this, put the pan on the stove and boil away the liquid until it turns clear and you only see a brown crust remaining covered with a layer of clear fat. You can then discard the fat and deglaze the pan.

At times we are confronted with more jus than we know what to do with. Well-roasted turkey (a euphemism for overcooked) will easily release 1 qt/960 ml of juices. When you take the cooked bird out of the pan, the pan will be full of liquid. You could, of course, decide to boil down the juices until they caramelize and the fat separates out as described earlier, but this is long and tedious and not necessarily the best option. Instead, separate the fat by putting the juices in a fat separator (basically a liquid measuring cup with the spout coming out of the bottom instead of the top) or in a glass pitcher and skim off the fat with a ladle.

Once you have your jus in hand, you may decide to make gravy. An old-fashioned gravy is especially welcome for turkey, for which a simple jus might seem a bit austere. Gravy is essentially a thickened jus. The usual thickener is flour, cooked with a little butter into a roux (see page 34), which gives the gravy its classic opaque appearance.

Sautéed Chicken

First, let it be said that butter is the secret to delicious sautéed chicken. When the chicken cooks in butter—whole butter is best, there is no need for clarifying it—the milk solids from the butter cling to the chicken and flavor it. If the cooking is carefully controlled, these milk solids caramelize and become deep brown and aromatic. Little fat is absorbed by the chicken. In fact, you'll be left with more fat in the pan than you started with.

When sautéing chicken, it's especially important that the pan be completely full of chicken or the butter will burn over any uncovered patches. [1] Another trick that ensures that the breast and thigh cook at the same time is to remove the thighbone and the drumstick. This speeds up the cooking of the thigh. [2] It's also a nice decorative touch to cut the nubs off the ends of the legs.

For one cut-up chicken, heat 3 tablespoons of unsalted butter in a heavy-bottomed skillet. When the butter begins to froth, slide in the chicken parts, skin-side down. Move the pan rapidly back and forth such that the chicken slides around a bit and doesn't stick. [3] Sauté over medium heat until the fat in the chicken skin renders and mixes with the butter in the pan. Cook until golden brown, about 15 minutes.

[4] Turn the chicken over and cook the flesh side. [5] Continue cooking until the chicken bounces back to the touch when pressed, about 5 minutes more.

When sautéing chicken, there are, of course, an unlimited number of sauce and garnish possibilities. [6] To make a sauce, pour the fat out of the pan and, if you like, add chopped shallots or garlic. [7] Deglaze the caramelized juices that adhere to the bottom of the pan with a generous splash of broth or water. Place the pan over medium-high heat and scrape the pan with a wooden spoon to dissolve the juices that have caramelized into a crust on the pan's surface. Either serve the resulting jus as is, or continue to add ingredients, such as white wine or chicken or vegetable stock with minced herbs and a pat of butter swirled in at the end, to turn it into a sauce. [8] The jus will be golden brown, a shade darker than the finished sautéed chicken.

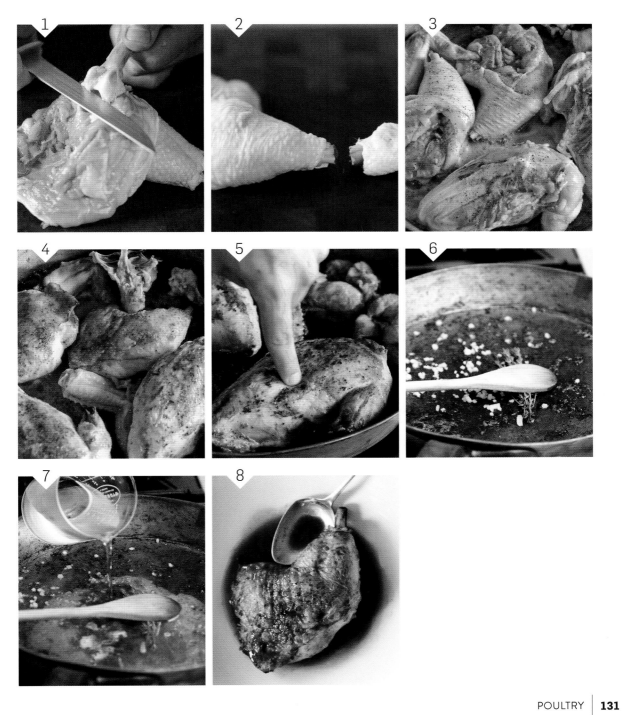

Grilled Chicken

There are a couple of approaches to grilling chicken. First, remove the thighbones from the two thighs (see page 131, photo 1) so they cook at the same time as the breast.

The major difficulty that faces the would-be chicken griller is the tendency of the fire to flare up as the fat from the chicken drips into the coals during cooking. There are those of us who like the bitter char that the flame imparts, but many don't like the soot that clings to chicken that has been exposed to flame. My first recommendation is to cook the chicken flesh-side down first (this runs counter to the directions in most books) while the fire is hottest. By the time the flesh side has browned, usually after about 15 minutes, the fire will have died down a little, making it less likely to flare up while you're grilling the skin side. If you have a gas grill, simply turn down the flame.

If the chicken starts to flare up when you turn it over, move the pieces around as soon as they flame. Another method is to build the fire on one side of the grill, use it to brown the chicken on both sides—if the fire is hot this can be accomplished in a few minutes—and then sort of "roast" the chicken by moving it away from the fire and covering the grill with the vents open.

[1] Just like sautéed chicken, grilled chicken—whether cooked on a grill pan or an actual grill—is done as soon as it's firm to the touch. If you're unsure of what this feels like, start by feeling the tip of the chicken breast. It will grow firm first while the rest of the breast is still fleshy. Gradually you will feel the stiffness work its way up to the thicker part of the breast. Once this fleshier part of the breast is stiff, the chicken is done.

Sautéed Skinless Boneless Chicken Breasts

My dinner guests always say I make the best chicken in the world. Whether I deserve these accolades or not, it must be said that I do nothing special—there are no fancy brines, marinades, or procedures. I just cook the breasts using a simple and classic method. The secret to the whole thing is simply not overcooking the chicken.

First, a disclaimer: Chicken breasts are far better tasting when cooked on the bone and with the skin. If you're reluctant to do this—you don't want to eat the skin and/or don't want to deal with the bones before cooking—cook the chicken on the bone and with the skin and, using a kitchen towel to protect your hand, pull away the cooked bones and skin. The resulting boneless and skinless breast will be far tastier than if you had cooked it with the bones and skin already removed.

If you're using boneless and skinless breasts, one way to restore their flavor is to bread them and cook them in clarified butter. Of course, this doesn't make the chicken low-calorie, but it's so good no one will care. There are several tricks to successful breading and several kinds of breading. The easiest is to simply flour the chicken and then cook it in clarified butter (the result is called *à la meunière*). When flouring chicken or when cooking it with no coating at all, it should be sautéed over high heat to ensure that it will brown. Chicken that has been floured can also be dipped in beaten egg and then sautéed (*à la parisienne*), or it can be dipped in egg and then in bread crumbs (*à l'anglaise*). When either of these last two methods is used, the heat should be relatively low to avoid burning the coating. A couple of tips for using bread crumbs: Make sure they're fresh by making them yourself from dense-crumbed white bread (never buy them in a box). Lightly bake the crustless slices in a low oven just to dry them out very slightly (as though they're a day old) and work them through a drum sieve or strainer. This ensures the bread crumbs are very fine and, hence, will absorb a minimum of butter.

Continued >>

[1] Dip the cutlets in the beaten egg. **[2]** Dredge in bread crumbs to coat well. **[3]** Cook over medium heat in clarified butter. **[4]** When golden brown on the first side, turn the cutlets and cook the other side. **[5]** Determining the doneness of a breast either on the bone or off is essentially the same—the meat becomes stiff and resilient as it cooks. If you're unsure what this means, see "The Hand Test" (below) or, better yet, keep poking the chicken with a finger as it cooks. You'll notice that the tip of the breast gets firm before the thicker part. If you keep pressing the breast, you'll notice this stiffness working its way toward the thicker part of the chicken as the meat cooks. As soon as the chicken bounces back to the touch when pressed at the thickest part, it is ready.

Once the chicken has cooked, you can make chicken *à la grenobloise*, a simple dish with brown butter, parsley, lemon, capers, and croutons. **[6]** Pour out the cooked butter. Add fresh butter, parsley, croutons, lemons, and capers to the pan. Cook until the butter is frothy. **[7]** To serve, spoon the hot butter sauce over the toasty golden-brown cutlets.

The Hand Test

If you press on the muscle at the base of your thumb, it will feel much like raw or undercooked meat. As you make a fist and clench the muscle, you emulate the texture of cooked meat. As soon as meat reaches this stage, it is medium-rare.

Fried Chicken

Fried chicken is one of those quintessentially American foods that people always seem to love.

The basic coating for fried chicken is a simple dredging in flour. Slightly more complicated, but not much, is a batter of flour and water worked to the consistency of heavy cream. The best method is to make a simple batter of flour and water and add a pinch of yeast to it to incorporate carbon dioxide, which makes the batter crispy. Batters containing egg release a strong odor if even slightly overcooked. Panko bread crumbs, attached with some milk or beaten egg, also create a distinctively crunchy crust that has its aficionados.

The oil for fried chicken should be just hot enough to brown the batter while cooking the chicken all the way through. [1] Start the oil at about 350°F/175°C. When you add the chicken, it will lower the temperature to about 300°F/150°C, which is just about right. Dip one piece of chicken into the hot oil to see if it floats. If it floats, the oil is ready. Add the chicken a bit at a time until the oil is bubbling furiously but not threatening to overflow. The total cooking time should be between 10 and 15 minutes. If it's browning faster than that, reduce the heat. If, conversely, it isn't browning, increase the heat. If the oil is too hot, the batter will brown but the chicken will be raw inside. If the oil is not hot enough, the chicken will overcook by the time the batter browns. If you're cooking chicken off the bone, however, it cooks much more quickly, in about 3 minutes, and requires a higher frying temperature, about 370°F/190°C. To test for doneness, using a slotted spoon, lift out one piece of chicken and set it on a cutting board. Press the chicken with your fingertip; if it's firm to the touch and not at all slack, it's ready.

[2] Scoop the rest of chicken out of the oil with a spider or skimmer. [3] Let drain on paper towels. [4] Fried chicken breaded with panko crumbs will have a shaggy look when finished.

Sautéed Chicken Livers and Chicken Liver Mousse

Many of us who don't like livers from larger animals (for example, from calves) fully appreciate chicken livers. Perhaps it's because of their gentler flavor or their delicate texture, but they are delicious served on their own with a modest sauce (made by deglazing the pan with shallots, a little reduced broth, and perhaps some cognac or Armagnac), or worked into purées, stuffings, and mousses.

[1] Chicken livers should be cooked in oil or clarified butter (whole butter won't get hot enough) over very high heat so they brown before overcooking. Stand back when they are cooking because they do spatter. [2] The chicken livers are ready when thoroughly browned and when they spring back to the touch.

Once the chicken livers are cooked, serve them as they are, slice and serve them on miniature toasts as an hors d'oeuvre, or convert them into a delicate mousse.

[3] To make a mousse, remove the livers from the pan and pour out the hot oil you cooked them in. Add chopped shallots and a little thyme to the pan. (Juniper berries are also good.) [4] Add a small amount of Cognac, Armagnac, or another good-quality brandy. Ignite with a match, carefully return to the heat, and boil until the flames subside. [5] Purée the chicken livers with an equal amount of cold butter in a food processor. [6] Purée until smooth. Work the mixture through a strainer into a bowl. [7] Fold in an equal amount of whipped cream (see page 190). [8] The liver mousse will be fluffy and spreadable, perfect for serving with crackers or bread.

Roast Turkey

One afternoon, while sitting comfortably at my desk, I got a phone call from a woman, clearly upset, who declared that I ruined her Thanksgiving dinner. She had begun to carve the turkey, discovered pink where the thighbone joins the back, and thrown the whole turkey out.

Be forewarned. Properly cooked fowl is pink inside. I don't mean the color of raw or undercooked fowl—white-fleshed birds (chicken, turkey, quail, etc.) should never be undercooked so that any translucent sheen remains in the meat—but definitely pink meat, or even red in spots, is acceptable. However, this pinkness or redness is limited to the area where the thigh joins the rest of the bird, so if you're squeamish about it, eat another part of the turkey. If you cook the turkey so this area is brown, you're guaranteed an overcooked bird. (One trick: When the bird is ready, carve off the thighs and roast them in a hot oven for 20 minutes or so to finish browning them.)

[1] There are a couple of tricks to successfully roasting a turkey, or any fowl for that matter. Put the giblets (liver, heart, and lungs) and turkey neck on the bottom of the roasting pan with some coarsely chopped aromatic vegetables and place the turkey on top. This prevents sticking, cooks the giblets and neck, and provides aromatic support.

Take a very simple approach and avoid turning the bird around once it's in the oven. In fact, don't baste the turkey, and check on it as little as possible so the heat stays in the oven. [2] Cover the breast loosely with a sheet of buttered aluminum foil for the first 30 minutes of cooking. This slows down the cooking of the breast meat so you have more time to cook the thigh meat, which takes longer. This method assures that every part of the bird will be done at the same time.

How do we know when the turkey is done? [3] The most reliable method is to use an instant-read thermometer to measure the temperature where the thigh meets the breast; when it reads 140°F/60°C, you know the turkey is done. But what if you don't have a thermometer? There's always the lip method (see page 11), but you can also check the juices inside the turkey's cavity. As the turkey cooks, the juices go from cloudy, to clear streaked with red, to clear with no color, to clear streaked with brown.

Continued >>

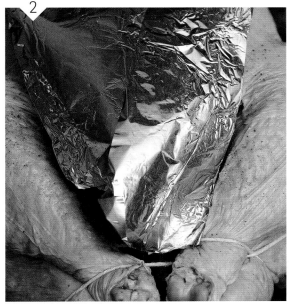

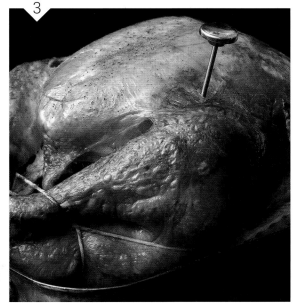

[4] The turkey is done when the juices are clear but still streaked with red. (Other sources say to cook until the juices are clear, but I find this overcooks the bird.) If you find that there are too few juices in the cavity for you to determine doneness, use a skewer to poke the side of the breast. Juices should run out and be clear, not streaked with red, as the juices in the cavity should be.

Once the turkey is done, you're probably going to want to make a jus or gravy. [5] A jus can simply be the juices that the bird has released during roasting, skimmed of their fat.

If you've cooked your turkey properly, you're going to be confronted with a paradox. When roasted correctly, a turkey releases very few juices with which to make a jus or gravy. You may find, in fact, that there are so few juices that you can't even skim off the fat. When confronted with not enough juices, boil down the juices you do have until they caramelize and leave a crust on the bottom of the pan. This allows you to pour off and discard the fat and deglaze the pan by pouring in 1 to 2 cups/240 to 480 ml store-bought or homemade broth or water. Once deglazed, scrape at the caramelized juices with a wooden spoon. At this point you can cook down the juices until they form a crust a second time, deglaze, and repeat ad infinitum to build a deeply flavored jus.

To make gravy, cook a little flour—2 tablespoons of flour per 2 cups/480 ml of gravy—in 2 tablespoons of melted butter or turkey fat to make a roux (see page 34). Add the jus to the roux and let simmer over low heat for 5 to 20 minutes to thicken. If you like, add the chopped giblets either raw or cooked.

Some people are fans of giblet gravy. There are two approaches to using giblets, one French, one Anglo-Saxon. I tend to use the Anglo-Saxon method for turkey and the French method for squab. When using the Anglo-Saxon method, the giblets are roasted with the turkey (as instructed in this entry). When the turkey is done, chop the giblets and any pieces from the neck to the consistency of hamburger relish. Stir these into the gravy just before serving. To use the French method, do not roast the giblets but instead chop the raw giblets with an equal amount of butter. Chop until very fine—in fact you might want to process the mixture in a food processor—and then whisk the hot jus into the giblet mixture just before serving. Gravy made the French way should have the consistency of loose mud.

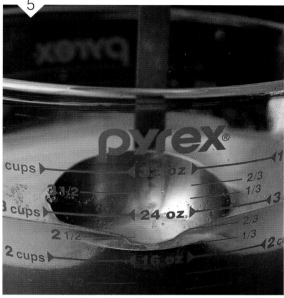

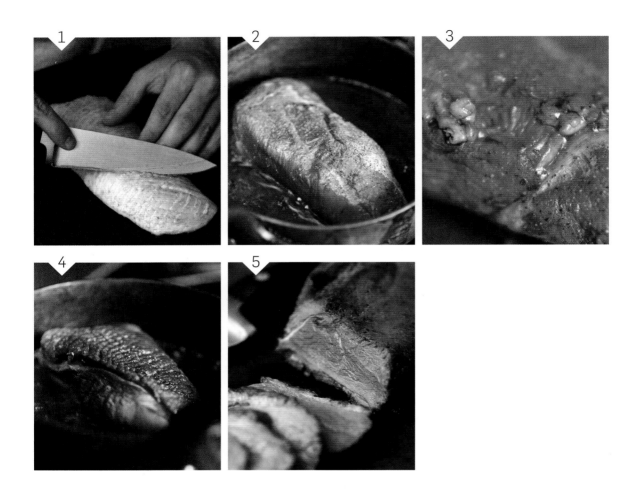

Sautéed Duck Breasts

Many of us hesitate to serve duck because we are intimidated. This is a pity since duck is a nice compromise between chicken and red meat. Duck is extremely versatile and is especially good with a sauce containing fruit or with sautéed fruits as a garnish. (I like to use apples or peaches, lightly sautéed in the fat rendered from the breast.)

A duck breast can be sautéed much like a steak, except that you must take the skin into consideration. Of course, you can remove the skin before cooking, which will yield a perfectly lean piece of meat (duck meat is leaner than chicken). But much of the flavor of a duck breast is in the skin; the fat in the skin also provides moisture and gives the breast a delightful crunch.

[1] Before sautéing, score the skin side of the breast with about 20 slices lengthwise and 20 more crosswise so you see a fine crosshatch pattern on the skin. When scoring, try to cut down as close to the meat as you can without actually cutting all the way through the skin.

[2] When sautéing duck breast, the trick is to do virtually all the sautéing on the skin side. This causes the fat to render and leaves the skin crispy while not overcooking the breast, which should be rare to medium-rare. Ideally, the fat will render and the skin will turn brown and crispy at the same time as the duck breast is cooked through. The rarer you want your duck, the higher the heat should be so that the skin browns before the duck cooks through. (Never cook a duck breast past medium.)

[3] Once the skin is brown and crispy and there's plenty of rendered fat in the pan, the breast should just be forming beads of juices along the side. If you start to see these juices form before the skin has browned, quickly increase the heat and brown the skin before the breast overcooks.

[4] When the skin has browned and you see the first juices form on the sides of the breast, turn the breast over and turn the heat to high. Brown for a minute or two and the breast is ready to serve. [5] To serve the breast, slice it on the diagonal.

PORK&
LAMB

Sautéed Bacon

We have a love-hate relationship with bacon. Few deny adoring it, yet it's filled with fat and smoke, which we all know isn't healthful. And yet, we can't resist it.

There are a couple of ways to cook bacon, the most traditional and typical is to sauté it in a heavy-bottomed skillet. It can also be baked in the oven (where it tends to spatter less and make less of a mess) or even cooked in the microwave, loosely covered with a paper towel to prevent spattering.

But regardless of how you cook bacon, it's important to know how to select it. Obviously it should be lean, but not so lean that there's nothing to crisp up. I like slab bacon (the whole piece of bacon from which slices are cut), because it keeps longer, and it also allows you to slice the bacon to any thickness you want.

Bacon should be cooked over gentle heat until it renders fat and begins to get crispy. The gentle heat is important so the bacon doesn't overbrown or even burn before it renders fat and becomes crispy. Bacon can be cooked to about three stages of doneness: only slightly rendered so the bacon remains flexible; more rendered until the bacon becomes crisp; and even more rendered until the bacon loses most of its fat and becomes brittle. While any of these stages makes for wonderful eating, nowadays people often opt for bacon cooked to at least the crispy stage, so that it has rendered more fat.

[1] Though we commonly buy bacon already sliced, it is better to start with a whole piece of slab bacon that you can cut yourself for optimal cooking. [2] Slide a knife along the bacon rind and separate it from the meat. [3] Continue cutting, keeping the knife against the rind, until you've completely removed it. [4] Slice the bacon to the thickness you like. Try to slice the bacon so the slices are of even thickness and will cook at the same time. (Of course, if you're using pre-sliced bacon, the slices will all be the same thickness.)

[5] Choose a heavy-bottomed skillet just large enough to hold the bacon in a single layer so the bacon cooks evenly. Cook the bacon over medium heat. If it starts to brown before it has rendered much of its fat, reduce the heat. [6] The bacon will be fatty and lightly browned when cooked to the first stage. [7] Most people like bacon cooked until it is crispy yet still full of delicious fat. [8] When most of the fat has rendered and the bacon is a deep red-brown, it is at its most-cooked stage, which is ideal for salads or other dishes, such as stews, that require a garnish.

Sautéed Sausage

Essentially ground meat stuffed into intestines, sausage is best sautéed. [1] It should be sautéed over low to medium heat. If the heat is too low, the sausage will over-cook without browning. Conversely, if the heat is too high, the casing will split, the meat juices will leak out, and the sausage will overbrown before it is cooked through. [2] Perfectly cooked sausage will be gently browned on the surface and hot in the center. [3] To determine doneness you can press the surface of the sausage to see if it springs back (indicating it is done) or you can slide an instant-read thermometer deep into its interior from one end. The inside temperature should be at least 140°F/60°C, but sausage is pretty forgiving (because of the fat it contains) if it gets hotter than that.

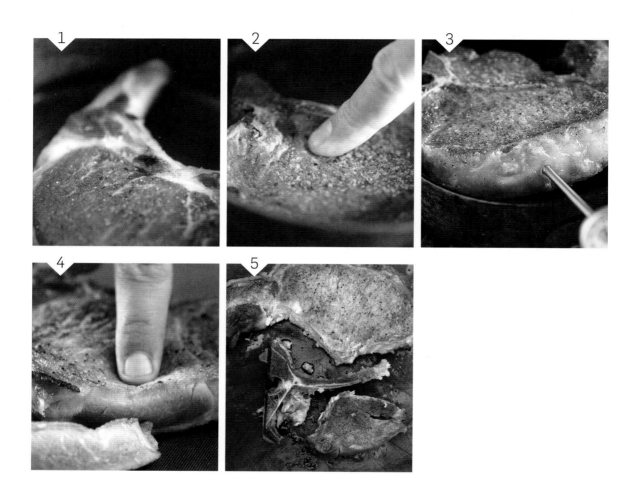

Sautéed Pork Chops

Before embarking on cooking your pork chops, keep in mind that most recommendations for proper cooking say to cook the chops to an internal temperature of 145°F/60°C. If you do this, your chops are going to be tough and dry. The proper temperature is closer to 130°F/54°C, which creeps up to 135°F/57°C as the chops rest. Don't, however, cook pork chops rare or medium-rare—they should always be medium.

When sautéing, there is, of course, always the consideration of which cooking fat to use. If your chops are especially thin, avoid using butter—the high heat necessary to brown the chops quickly will burn the butter. If you're cooking larger chops, which are cooked at a lower temperature than thinner ones, butter works fine. When using butter, however, the usual precautions apply. The pan should be full and you should watch the heat carefully to make sure the butter doesn't burn.

If you're not insistent that your chops taste buttery, go ahead and use oil. I use regular "pure" olive oil instead of extra-virgin olive oil, which is expensive.

Heat the pan with the oil in it until the oil begins to ripple. Add the chops and adjust the temperature according to how thick they are—the thicker the chop, the lower the heat should be so it has time to penetrate without burning the outside of the chop. Like virtually all meat, pork becomes firm and resilient to the touch as it cooks, so your best bet for determining doneness is simply to press on top of the chop and feel if it bounces back. If the chops are especially large this can be difficult, as the thick outer part of the chop obscures the texture of the middle, where the cooking is taking place. [1] When juices start to form on the top and sides of the chop, in 5 to 10 minutes, flip it over. [2] When the surface of the second side bounces back to the touch when pressed, usually about 5 minutes after you turned the chops, the chop is done. [3] You can also determine if the chop is done by sliding a thermometer in through the side to the center and seeing if it measures the requisite 130°F/54°C. [4] A chop is underdone when it is still fleshy. [5] When the loin and tenderloin are separated you can easily see the distinctive shapes of the two muscles that comprise a loin chop.

Braised Pork Shoulder Chops

Pork (or veal) shoulder chops come from closer toward the head on the animal than do the neat center-cut chops we usually sauté or grill. Because they contain fat and gristle, they are less expensive and take less well to grilling and sautéing. But this same fat and gristle make them perfect for braising. Once braised, the braising liquid can be finished with herbs or garnished with such traditional foods as lightly stewed prunes or apricots. Don't try to braise center-cut chops or they'll dry out.

[1] To braise pork (or veal) shoulder chops, they must first be sautéed on both sides to brown them. [2] The fat in the pan is discarded and replaced with fresh fat or oil. [3] Aromatic vegetables are gently cooked (sweated) in the pan until soft. [4] The chops go back in the pan with a handful of herbs (bouquet garni), and enough liquid (white wine is good) is added to come halfway up the chops. The chops are covered loosely with aluminum foil and the lid is placed on top. [5] The chops are then simmered for about 1 hour, until a carving fork or paring knife slides easily in and out of the chop without the chop clinging to the carving fork.

[6] When the chops are done, the braising liquid is strained into a saucepan to reduce and the fat is skimmed off with a ladle. Serve the juices over the braised chops or, if you like, glaze the chops by putting them in a 400°F/200°C oven with their braising liquid and basting them.

Roasted Leg of Lamb

A leg of lamb makes a nice compromise roast—cheaper than veal or an expensive cut of beef or lamb (such as the rack or saddle)—and it's a generous size. A typical American leg of lamb serves approximately 10 people.

The roasting is pretty basic: The leg is allowed to come to room temperature and is roasted in a 500°F/260°C oven, to properly brown it, for the first 20 minutes of cooking. Then the temperature is lowered to 300°F/150°C to ensure even cooking for the remainder of the cooking time. If you want to use a *fonçage*—a base of meat trimmings and/or vegetables—you'll have to buy 1 to 2 lb/455 to 910 g of lamb stew meat since your roast won't provide much in the way of trimmings. You can cut the vegetables into rather large pieces since they'll have plenty of time to roast—at least an hour. In fact, a roast leg of lamb presents the perfect opportunity for roasting vegetables. By placing the vegetables under and around the roast, they absorb fats and juices and take on a rich flavor.

Because of its shape and because it's rather large, a leg of lamb won't be done evenly. In other words, the meat around the shank may approach medium while the rest of the roast is rare. This is usually more of a convenience than anything because with a crowd of 10 people there are going to be different requests for degrees of doneness. To know when your roast is done, insert a thermometer or skewer into the meat at the thickest part. When the roast registers 120°F/48°C, it's rare; 125°F/52°C is medium-rare; and 130°F/54°C degrees is medium. These temperatures are the actual temperature of the meat when you take the reading. Keep in mind that they increase about 5°F/3°C as the roast rests.

If you don't have a meat thermometer and you haven't mastered the lip method, you'll have to judge doneness by appearance. I tend to like leg of lamb cooked more than most meat—medium-rare instead of rare—but of course this is purely a matter of taste. [1] To judge the doneness, notice how the meat contracts around the shank and exposes bone. Sometimes the meat is trimmed off the shank for presentation, but you can still see how the meat has contracted by looking closely at the meat on the bone. [2] When blood begins to form on the surface of the roast, the heat is penetrating into the middle. When this begins, the meat is rare but will quickly move to medium-rare. Notice also the formation of juices on the bottom of the pan. If you want your roast rare, take it out after the appearance of a tablespoon or so of juices. For medium-rare, wait until there are more juices, say several tablespoons. As the roast continues to cook it will release more juices. If you cook the roast all the way to medium (which isn't fatal for a leg of lamb like it might be for other roasts), you'll have a panful of tasty juices with which to make a sauce.

When the roast is done, transfer it to a platter and cover it loosely with aluminum foil. Prepare the jus. If there are a lot of juices—more than 1 cup/240 ml or so—transfer them to a measuring cup or fat separator (see "What Is a Fat Separator," page 159) and skim off most of the fat. [3] If you have less meat juice, leave the roasting vegetables in the pan and boil down the juices on top of the stove until they caramelize and form a crust on the bottom of the pan. Pour or spoon off the fat and deglaze the pan with a little water, broth, or white wine. Typically white wine is a little strong for a jus, but combined with equal parts water or broth, it lends a crisp bit of acidity.

Remember that a leg of lamb has two sides, one thicker than the other. Typically, the thinner side cooks faster, so if you have guests who want their meat more or less done, keep this in mind. [4] When you carve meat off the thinner side of the roast, the meat on top is more done and becomes rarer as you work toward the center of the roast. [5] On the thicker side, the meat is less done. [6] As you work toward the center, the meat gets more rare.

Continued >>

What Is a Fat Separator?

There are a number of methods for separating the fat that floats to the top of broths and gravies. A small spoon or ladle works well enough for skimming fat off the surface, but a fat separator is best. A fat separator is simply a glass or plastic pitcher with the spout coming out the bottom rather than the top. This way, when you pour, the broth or gravy comes out of the spout and the liquid fat remains behind.

Roasted Rack of Lamb

A rack of lamb makes a beautiful roast. It cooks quickly (in about 25 minutes) and is impressive to present and carve. It is a memorable alternative to a crown roast, which looks more dramatic than it tastes (see "Crown Roasts," page 163).

The only thing about rack of lamb is that, in most cases, it requires some prep. If you buy a rack of lamb that comes from New Zealand or Australia, it will come in Cryovac (thick clear plastic) and will have already been trimmed and *frenched*, which simply means that the bones are trimmed of meat and fat so they protrude dramatically above the roast. Racks from Down Under are smaller than American racks, so much so that one rack typically serves only two (racks have eight rib chops).

American racks are larger—one rack serves four—and usually need some trimming. They can also be frenched. Very few American butchers know how to do this, and it's somewhat time-consuming, so it's a good thing to learn how to do yourself (see my book *Essentials of Cooking* for a detailed explanation). When you buy an American rack, make sure that the spinal column, called the *chine bone*, has been removed.

Once you have a trimmed rack, it can be roasted in the usual way. Keep in mind that the roasting time is short, so any aromatic vegetables (such as carrots, onions, fennel, and turnips) added to the roasting pan should be cut smallish so they cook in time. (You can also pre-roast the vegetables.) Allow the meat to come to room temperature before roasting. [1] Spread the slices of meat trimmings in a small roasting pan over the aromatic vegetables. [2] Roast the trimmings and vegetables in a 500°F/260°C oven for about 15 minutes.

[3] Put the rack on top of the bed of meat trimmings and vegetables. Slide into the oven. Roast for about 20 minutes and then begin checking for doneness.

[4] To determine doneness, press on both ends of the rack at the same time. When the rack is resilient and resists pressure (in other words, when it feels firm) it is done or almost done. [5] To confirm that it's done, press on the center of the rack to see if the meat feels firm. Usually the meat in the center firms up about 5 minutes after the ends. [6] The finished rack of lamb will appear well browned with juices forming on the surface.

[7] To prepare the jus, boil down any juices left in the pan, and discard the fat. [8] Add broth or water to the roasting pan and scrape the bottom of the pan with a wooden spoon. [9] To serve the rack, slice between each rib. [10] Serve the slices of rack with the jus.

Continued >>

Crown Roasts

There are those for whom a crown roast, made by taking two or more racks of lamb or pork and bending them around so they form a crownlike shape, is the very apotheosis of fine dining. The inherent problem with this method is that you have to cut slits in the roast between the ribs to allow it to bend. These slits, right in the loin muscle, expose the meat and may cause it to release precious juices during roasting. My recommendation is to stick to an elegant and simple rack instead.

9

10

BEEF

Grilled Porterhouse

A porterhouse is a cross section of the back of the animal and includes not only the strip (in some parts of the country called a *New York cut*) but also the tenderloin, sometimes called the *filet mignon*. Hence, there are two muscles, each with their own characteristics, separated by a T-shaped bone. When the area of the piece of tenderloin diminishes in size, the steak is called a *T-bone*.

Because there is a lot of meat on a porterhouse, it's best made for at least two people. A porterhouse steak butchered thin enough for just one serving will be thin indeed—too thin. Count on 1 lb/455 g per two people; if you're making a porterhouse for four, it should weigh at least 2 lb/910 g.

[1] When choosing your porterhouse, be prepared to spend a lot of money. Don't skimp and buy something cheap—if you're strapped it's better to buy a good-quality cheaper cut—or you'll be wasting your money. Ideally the steak should be prime grade and well marbled. It should also be dry-aged for at least a month. To find a porterhouse that meets these specifications, you're going to have to go to a good butcher. Don't ever marinate a porterhouse or you'll interfere with the delicacy of the meat. [2] Make sure the steak is at room temperature before you start grilling or it will be overdone on the outside and raw in the middle.

Steaks are more complicated to cook than chops because there are multiple levels of doneness instead of just one, as there is for pork or veal chops. The rarer you want the meat, the hotter the fire should be. I recommend rare to medium-rare. If you're cooking the steak black and blue—essentially browned on the outside and raw inside—or very rare, simply brown it for about 2 minutes on each side. If it's extremely thick, the fire should be lower and the steak grilled for more like 3 minutes on each side. When grilling very rare, or black and blue, keep in mind that the steak won't really do anything to indicate doneness—it won't stiffen or form many juices. [3] A porterhouse cooked rare appears well browned and juices will have formed near or on the bones after 2 to 3 minutes. This indicates that it's time to flip the steak. Cook the steak for about 2 minutes on the second side, just long enough to brown it.

[4] A medium-rare porterhouse is distinguished by the fact that it bounces back to the touch and shows more red juices than a steak cooked rare. If you're cooking the steak to a genuine medium-rare—be careful to not go beyond this degree of doneness—cook it long enough to see juices forming on the meat, not just on the bones. When you see these juices, the meat is ready to be turned. Grill for about 3 minutes on the second side.

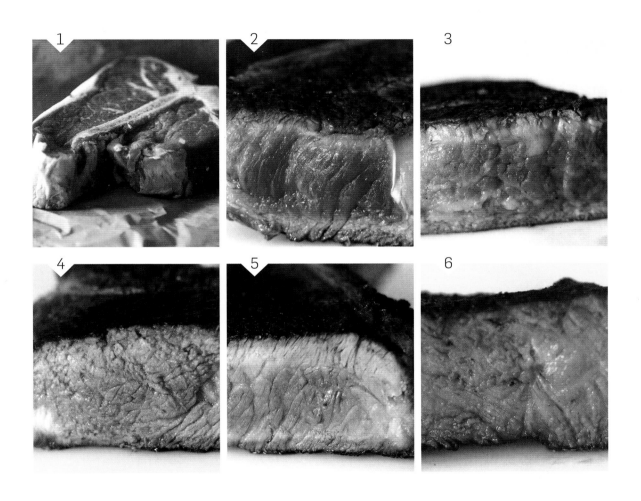

[5] Medium porterhouse bounces back to the touch and releases plenty of red or pink juices. [6] The well-done porterhouse is denoted by its copious brown juices and firm texture.

Since porterhouse is not an individual steak, you'll have to carve it. Cut along the bone to detach both the round tenderloin and the strip. Slice each of these and give everyone a little of each.

Grilled or Sautéed Hamburgers

It may seem paradoxical—after all, hamburgers are supposed to be easy—but hamburgers are among the hardest foods for which to determine doneness. This may be because their original structure is broken down when the meat is chopped.

Hamburgers are best cooked on a hot grill or sautéed in a heavy-bottomed pan on the stove over medium-high heat. When looking for doneness, watch closely for blood and juice formation on the surface, which indicates that the heat is penetrating the center. To some degree you can also tell by feel—when the hamburger bounces back when pressed with a finger, it's medium-rare.

[1] Brown 1-in-/2.5-cm-thick burgers on both sides. [2] For black-and-blue burgers—which are essentially raw in the middle—brown the meat over medium to high heat for 90 seconds on each side and let rest for 2 minutes. At this point the meat will be soft to the touch and there will be no formation of juices. [3] For a rare burger, cook for about 2 ½ minutes on each side and let rest for 2 minutes. You should see just the beginning of the formation of juices. [4] After 3 ½ minutes on each side, clear juices should start to run out of the burger, which indicates medium-rare. [5] When blood turns brown and starts to run out in copious amounts, the hamburger has reached medium. When it's well done, after about 7 minutes on each side, the juices will be entirely brown and the surface of the burger will feel hard to the touch. Let all burgers rest for 2 minutes before assembling and serving.

Beef Stew

A stew is simply a braise in which meat or seafood has been cut into bite-size pieces.

Typically the meat is marinated in wine or some other flavorful liquid (for example, cider or beer) along with aromatic vegetables, especially onions and carrots. An elegant and welcome touch is a strip of fatback carefully slid into each piece of meat. This ensures that each piece will have a moist center.

Most recipes call for browning the meat, but this isn't necessary. It does help bring out the caramelized flavor of the browned meat, but does little to affect tenderness or moistness.

As for all braises, stews must be cooked at a bare simmer so that the fat that's released floats to the top instead of getting churned back into the braising liquid. Once the meat is tender and can be easily crushed between two fingers, it should be gently transferred to a new pot and the braising liquid strained into a saucepan, where it can be reduced slightly and degreased. Once degreased, the liquid can be thickened, either with cornstarch (diluted in an equal amount of water) or beurre manié, which is simply a paste of equal parts flour and room-temperature butter. When using either of these, the liquid must come back to a boil for the thickening to take effect.

When the sauce is ready, it should be recombined with the meat and the meat reheated. At this point, garnishes such as mushrooms, pearl onions, lardons (strips of bacon about 1 in/2.5 cm long and ¼ in/6 mm wide), turned carrots or turnips (see "Turned Vegetables," page 68), and other vegetables, each cooked in the manner most appropriate for it, can be added.

[1] I use short ribs because of their high fat content, which helps keep them moist. The only downside to this is their expense. [2] Marinate the stew meat with aromatic vegetables, a bundle of herbs (bouquet garni), and wine in the refrigerator for 4 hours, or as long as overnight.

[3] For speed and optimal tenderness, I like to cook the stew in a pressure cooker at maximum pressure but without allowing any steam to escape through the safety valve (see "Braising with a Pressure Cooker," page 18). [4] Test the meat for doneness. If the stew meat clings to a skewer, it isn't ready.

Continued >>

[5] The stew is ready when you can easily crush a piece of meat between your fingers. [6] To thicken the stewing liquid, work equal parts butter and flour into a smooth paste (beurre manié). [7] Notice that the unthickened stewing liquid doesn't coat (or in professional lingo, nap) a spoon dipped in it. [8] Grab a glob of the beurre manié with a whisk and whisk the paste into the boiling stewing liquid. [9] Notice how the thickened liquid now coats, or naps, a spoon.

[10] Once you have your basic stew, you can add any number of ingredients, especially vegetables, to give it variety. I like to use glazed pearl onions (see page 72) and carrots (see page 56), bacon lardons, and sautéed mushrooms (see page 74). [11] The thickened stewing liquid will lightly coat the tender stew meat and vegetables.

Pot Roast

A pot roast isn't a roast but rather a braise, a long brown braise to be exact. The most critical part of cooking a pot roast is to obtain a cut fatty enough so that the meat won't dry out during the long cooking. I prefer the chuck blade roast, which is usually well marbled and has plenty of fat to keep it moist.

[1] Of course if you're fanatical about making the perfect pot roast, you'll want to lard the meat (see "Larding," page 177) to ensure that it doesn't dry out. [2] When the roast is larded, marinate it with aromatic vegetables, a bundle of herbs (bouquet garni), and wine in the refrigerator for 4 hours, or as long as overnight. [3] Remove the roast from the marinade, pat it dry, and brown it in oil in the roasting pan over high heat. Transfer the roast to a platter. [4] Brown the carrots and onions. [5] Fit the browned vegetables and meat into the pot and add enough liquid to come halfway up the meat. If the pot fits very closely, go ahead and cover the meat.

Once the liquid has been added to the meat, cover the pot and simmer over low heat. I like to use a pressure cooker (see "Braising with a Pressure Cooker," page 18), which cooks a 4-lb/1.8-kg piece of meat in 45 minutes. Of course pressure cookers vary so you'll want to follow the manufacturer's directions. [6] Pressure cookers all have some type of switch—on mine, it's the small yellow button—that indicates when the maximum pressure has been reached. Maintain the cooking with the button up, but don't allow the pressure cooker to hiss.

Continued >>

[7] When the meat is properly cooked, a carving fork or knife inserted into the meat will slide easily in and out with little resistance. At this point, the braising liquid should be strained and carefully and thoroughly degreased, and the vegetables picked out and discarded. [8] The pot roast should then be placed in a smaller pot or pan to compensate for the fact that it will have shrunk, the degreased braising liquid poured over it, and the whole thing roasted in a 400°F/200°C oven for about 30 minutes while basting every 5 minutes until the meat is covered with a shiny glaze. [9] Present the pot roast with the braising liquid poured over it. [10] The roast should be tender enough to serve with two spoons.

Larding

It may seem crazy, in this lean meat–obsessed age, to intentionally work fat into meat, but meat that is too lean will dry out when braised. Don't follow the mistaken notion that a moist cooking method helps keep meat moist; it does not. It is fat that keeps meat from drying out.

Since meat is getting leaner and leaner, and cuts such as veal shoulder are lean to begin with, it becomes necessary to insert strips of pork fat, called *fatback*, into the meat before cooking. To do this, you need a few things. First you need to find the fatback. It is sold in two forms—in neat little squares or rectangles with a thick layer of fat and a rind (the more desirable option), or in sheets with a thinner and less regular layer of fat. Unfortunately, the latter form is easier to find than the first. (My butcher said he would need me to buy 60 lb/27 kg in order to get the good fatback.) Whichever kind you end up with, remove the rind by sliding a long, thin, and very sharp knife between the fat and rind. Save the rind to add to your braises (it provides gelatin) and cut the fat into strips about 5 in/12 cm long and ¼ in/6.5 mm wide.

Once you have your strips of fatback, you need to insert them into the meat. There are two implements for accomplishing this, a larder and an interlarder, although most people call them both larders. A larder is a tube with a handle on it. The tube is open along one side. You simply place a piece of fat in the tube and slide the tube into the meat. You then hold the fat in place while you pull out the tube.

I often find it easier to use an interlarder than a larder. An interlarder looks a little like a knitting needle with a serrated hinge on the back end. To use it, attach a strip of fat with the hinge and drag it through the meat. Release the hinge once you've pulled the strip of fat through. Both larders and interlarders are available at well-stocked kitchen supply stores.

Braised or Poached Oxtails

Very few foods are as savory as braised or poached oxtails, which may explain why they now appear on restaurant menus everywhere. Typically home cooks hesitate to make them, perhaps because oxtails take so long to cook—upward of 5 hours—or possibly because they are unsure how to achieve that savory perfection at home. Oxtails present a good excuse to use a pressure cooker (see "Braising with a Pressure Cooker," page 18). If you don't have a pressure cookier, follow the same process described here, but using a heavy-bottomed pot, uncovered; braise for approximately 4 hours. In addition to making basic braised oxtails, you can layer the meat and braising liquid in a terrine (a mold), and then slice and serve it like a pâté.

[1] Start by buying the largest pieces of oxtail you can find. [2] Brown the oxtails on both sides in oil and set aside. Discard the oil. [3] In fresh oil, sweat coarsely chopped aromatic vegetables until they soften. [4] Add wine to deglaze the pan. [5] Put the oxtails and aromatic vegetables in the pressure cooker. Add a bundle of herbs (bouquet garni) and whatever remaining liquid you're using, such as broth. I like to use wine for the deglazing and additional broth (or water in a pinch) to cover the oxtails. Bring the pressure cooker up to pressure and maintain over low heat so that the button indicates it's under pressure but you do not hear hissing, which would mean boiling that could cloud the broth. If you're making basic braised oxtails, start checking them after 20 minutes. Poke between the meat and the bone with a fork and see if you can pull the meat away. If not, keep cooking. If you're using the oxtails for a soup or terrine, cook them until the meat is falling off the bone and offers no resistance when you pull it away with a fork.

Continued >>

[6] Chill the oxtails and braising liquid in the refrigerator overnight. Spoon off and discard the fat. For basic braised oxtails, strain and reduce the braising liquid, adding a generous splash of sherry and red wine to make a concentrated sauce. Warm the braised oxtails in the sauce, then scoop into soup plates and serve.

For a terrine, first melt the braising liquid (it will have congealed) if it isn't already warm, and then go through and separate the meat from the rest of the ingredients. Discard the bones and reserve everything else. Strain the braising liquid. Pour a layer of the warm braising liquid into the bottom of the terrine. Refrigerate for about 10 minutes or until this first layer is set. [7] Spoon a layer of meat over the set braising liquid. [8] Pour in enough braising liquid (make sure it's cold but not set or it will melt the liquid you've already added) to cover the meat. Refrigerate until set, usually for about 10 minutes. [9] Continue layering in this way until the terrine is filled. Allow the whole terrine to set for a couple of hours in the refrigerator. (The terrine should be kept refrigerated and will last for about a week.)

[10] Dip the terrine in a bowl of hot water for about 30 seconds to loosen it and unmold it onto a platter. Slice to serve. (You can also leave it in the mold and cut the slices out of the pan.)

Osso Buco

Veal shank, otherwise known as osso buco, makes a perfect braise. You can buy the whole shank—a whole shank serves about four people—or you can buy it in slices, typically about 1½ in/4 cm thick. In any case, the process of braising osso buco is simple: The meat is browned and wine, broth, and a bundle of herbs (bouquet garni) are added. The meat is then braised at a low heat until easily penetrated with a knife or fork.

As with all braises, osso buco should include aromatic vegetables such as onions and carrots. Typically, these vegetables are chopped and lightly browned in the same pot used to brown the veal. They are then cooked along with the veal and strained out at the end. However, if the aromatic vegetables are cut in a decorative way, they can be left in. I use leeks, carrots, and turnips cut into julienne, or thin strips. The meat is braised for an hour or so and the vegetables are added. The braise continues, the vegetables soften, and the flavors marry. When the osso buco is ready to serve, the vegetables should be melting and soft and mounded up over the meat so they can be eaten at the same time.

[1] For cooking slices of osso buco, brown the slices of veal on both sides in a heavy pot over high heat. [2] Discard the burnt fat, put the veal back in the pot with its bouquet garni, and pour the wine, broth, or other braising liquid over it. Cover the pot and braise over low heat for about 1 hour. [3] Add the julienned vegetables. Cover the pot and braise for about 1 hour more. [4] Poke the veal to see if a fork penetrates it easily, indicating the meat is done. [5] If the veal grips on to the fork when lifted, the meat is not done. [6] Serve the tender osso buco with a pile of the cooked vegetables on top.

Braised or Sautéed Sweetbreads

The meat we are accustomed to eating is usually muscle, but animals also provide an array of tasty organs, such as the liver, spleen, kidneys, heart, and, best of all, sweetbreads, which have become increasingly popular in the past decade. Though they may seem challenging to cook, sweetbreads are more easily prepared than you might think.

Sweetbreads are the thymus gland and pancreas. [1] The thymus is a neat oval, while the pancreas is a rather messy stringy part. Be sure to buy your sweetbreads from a reputable butcher. Some places only sell the pancreas and sell off the nice rounds (the thymus) to buyers in Europe. You want as high a percentage of the round thymus as possible.

When properly cooked, sweetbreads have a firm but very tender consistency and the flavor of the freshest veal. It's imperative not to overcook them or they'll dry out. They are properly cooked as soon as they spring back to the touch.

Before sweetbreads are cooked, they need to be blanched and then weighted down, which helps them keep their shape. [2] To blanch the sweetbreads, put them in a pot with just enough cold water to cover. Place on high heat and bring to a simmer. Immediately drain and transfer to a baking sheet. [3] While they're still hot, weight the sweetbreads down with a heavy cutting board and a heavy pan or other heavy object placed on top. [4] Refrigerate the sweetbreads until set, about 5 hours. The blanched sweetbreads will have a somewhat flabby, raw texture when you poke them with your finger.

Once the sweetbreads have been blanched and weighted down, you can cook them in one of two ways. They can be gently sautéed or braised and sliced relatively thickly. When sautéed, they are best when floured or breaded like chicken (see page 133). [5] Slice the weighted sweetbreads into strips about ½ in/12 mm thick. [6] Flour or bread the strips. [7] Sauté the strips in butter or clarified butter until they are firm and bounce back to the touch.

The most typical approach for braising sweetbreads is to sweat finely diced carrots, onions, and celery; place the sweetbreads on top; add liquid such as broth; cover with parchment paper or aluminum foil; and braise in the oven. The mistake most people make, however, is to add too much liquid, which dilutes the flavor of the sweetbreads and makes the sauce insipid. A better method is to leave out the braising liquid entirely and rely on the juices released by the sweetbreads to create the sauce.

Gently sauté (sweat) cubes of carrots, onions, and celery (mirepoix) on the stove until tender, about 15 minutes. **[8]** Put the sweetbreads on top of the mirepoix. Notice how I use a pan that's just the size of the sweetbreads and not bigger, which promotes even and efficient cooking. **[9]** Place a round of parchment paper or aluminum foil over the sweetbreads, which helps trap in steam so the sweetbreads cook evenly but still allows for evaporation and concentration of the braising liquid. **[10]** Check the sweetbreads after about 15 minutes. If the mixture has begun to dry out, add a small amount (¼ cup/60 ml) of broth or other liquid. The sweetbreads are ready when they spring back to the touch, after about 20 minutes. **[11]** The concentrated juices and mirepoix are converted to a sauce with the addition of a splash of cream.

Continued >>

SWEETS & BREADS

Whipped Cream

Much like beaten egg whites, whipped cream is used in many things. As with beaten egg whites, heavy cream goes through various stages as it's beaten—going from soft to medium and then stiff peaks. If you beat it long enough, it ultimately turns into butter.

[1] To whip cream, make sure the heavy cream is ice-cold before beating. If it's very hot in the kitchen, beat the cream over a bowl of ice. After whipping the cream for 2 to 3 minutes, soft peaks will form. [2] After whipping the cream, for a minute or two more, stiff peaks will form. [3] If you overwhip the cream, you will end up with butter. [4] Unless you're using the butter right away, you'll need to remove the buttermilk (because it turns rancid in a day or two). To remove the buttermilk, knead the butter in a bowl of cool (but not ice cold) water until it is smooth and malleable, changing the water until it remains clear during the kneading.

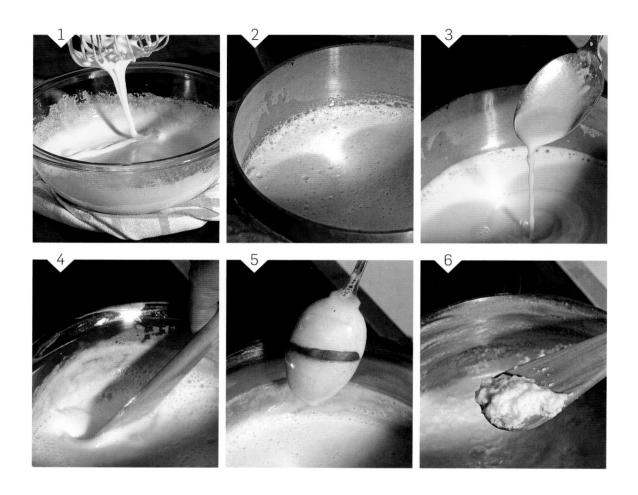

Crème Anglaise

Otherwise known as custard cream, crème anglaise is a combination of milk, sugar, and egg yolks, usually flavored with vanilla, that's cooked slowly on the stove until it takes on a silky, slightly thicker consistency. Because it contains no flour, it must never be allowed to come to a boil or it will curdle.

Crème anglaise terrifies people because it can be particularly difficult to determine when it's done. This challenge is exacerbated by the fact that if you overcook the custard, even for a second, it will curdle. To some degree this can be reversed—by immediately puréeing the custard in a blender—but the resulting custard won't be quite the same as classic crème anglaise.

One helpful thing to know: The slower you cook the custard, the more stable the egg yolks become and the greater the range of temperatures the custard can tolerate before the crème anglaise curdles.

The standard way to determine doneness is to stand there stirring the custard with a wooden spoon, constantly checking how the custard clings to the spoon. The custard is done when a streak made through the custard on the back of the spoon with your finger stays in place. The problem with this method is that it's hard to tell when the streak looks exactly right. I've seen students standing there, examining their spoons, while the crème anglaise sits on the flame and curdles. When making crème anglaise, you can't stop stirring, even for a second.

A better method is to look closely just at the custard's consistency. When you start stirring, you'll see lots of little ripples form around the spoon. But as soon as the crème anglaise is done, these ripples disappear and are replaced with thicker, silky waves. As soon as you see this, take the cream off the heat and continue stirring for about 5 minutes until it cools. (If you let it sit there without stirring, it may curdle.)

[1] Whisk together sugar and egg yolks in a bowl until pale, about 3 minutes. [2] Add boiling milk to the egg yolk mixture while whisking constantly and return this mixture to the saucepan used for heating the milk. [3] Notice the consistency of the milk–egg yolk mixture before it is cooked. [4] Stir the cream with a wooden spoon over low to medium heat until it takes on a silky consistency. [5] The crème anglaise is done when you can make a line on the back of a spoon with your finger and it stays there. [6] When overcooked, the crème anglaise curdles and looks like scrambled eggs and water. Properly cooked crème anglaise has a magnificent silky consistency that coats the mouth without being at all gluey or starchy.

Zabaglione

The great thing about zabaglione is that you can make it with things most of us usually have around the house—wine and eggs—and, when served in tall glasses, it makes a dramatic impression. I like to spoon it over berries, but classically it is served alone.

Zabaglione is a foamy emulsion made with Marsala, Madeira, or sherry combined with egg yolks. (When made with white wine, it's called a sabayon.) The mixture is much like a crème anglaise, except that wine replaces the milk and instead of stirring with a spoon to prevent froth, we beat it with a whisk to incorporate as much air as possible. The zabaglione is done when it boils.

"Boils?" you may ask. Yes, despite the fact that egg yolks curdle when they get too hot, what you see boiling is actually the alcohol contained in the wine, which boils at a lower temperature than water. So when the zabaglione boils, the egg yolks will have played their role as thickening agents, setting the mixture.

[1] Combine the egg yolks with sugar and wine and beat over medium heat. [2] As you continue beating, you'll notice the liquid taking on volume and becoming frothy. [3] As the zabaglione cooks, it will lose some volume. You can verify that the zabaglione is done by dipping in a spoon and making a line with your finger to see if it leaves an impression. [4] Well-made zabaglione sets into a luxurious, unctuous foam.

Pastry Cream

Pastry cream is a little bit like crème anglaise—hot milk cooked with egg yolks—except that a thickener such as flour or cornstarch is added to the egg yolks before they are combined with the milk. This thickener stabilizes the egg yolks so they don't curdle, even when you boil the mixture. In fact, you have to boil the mixture in order for the thickener to work.

Pastry cream is useful for all manner of things—filling profiteroles, making napoleons, and as a cake filling. When used as a cake filling, butter is often beaten into the pastry cream, turning it into a mousseline. No matter what you're using the pastry cream for, you can work a small amount of clarified butter into the cream to give it a buttery flavor.

[1] To make pastry cream, beat egg yolks and flour or cornstarch until smooth in a stainless-steel or glass bowl. Scrape the miniature seeds out of a split vanilla bean and add them to the milk. Bring the milk to a boil and pour it into the egg yolks–flour mixture. Return this mixture to the pan and continue cooking, stirring constantly, over medium heat. [2] Notice how the pastry cream turns very pale yellow and froths up while it's cooking. [3] When the pastry cream is done, it will come to a boil and be thick. [4] Add richness and flavor by whisking in clarified butter.

Buttercream Frosting

Buttercream is a rich filling used for cakes. While it's basically a mixture of sugar and butter, there are several ways to make it. The most common approach, at least among amateur bakers, is simply to beat together powdered sugar and butter and some kind of flavoring such as coffee or chocolate. Real aficionados, however, find buttercream made in this way to have a subtly gritty consistency from the cornstarch contained in the sugar.

Professionals use one of three methods: beating cold butter with crème anglaise, beating cold butter into Italian meringue (the soft meringue used as an icing for cakes) or room-temperature butter into previously made meringue, and cooking egg yolks with sugar syrup cooked to the soft-ball stage (see page 203). The last method is how most bakers make buttercream. Once the egg yolks are cooked and beaten with the sugar syrup, butter is added and the mixture beaten until smooth. The flavoring is added at the very end.

There are a couple of things to keep in mind when making buttercream in this way. First, the eggs, still in their shells, should be warmed in a bowl of hot water before you separate them. This ensures that cold egg yolks don't cool the hot sugar syrup. When pouring the syrup into the bowl, avoid letting it hit the sides of the mixing bowl or the whisk. Otherwise, the syrup congeals into little globules that can end up in the finished buttercream.

[1] Whisk egg yolks in the bowl of an electric mixer on medium speed for a couple of minutes, until they turn pale yellow. Pour the soft-ball sugar syrup into the egg yolks, doing your best to avoid letting the syrup hit the whisk or the sides of the bowl. Once you've added all the sugar syrup, increase the mixer speed to high. [2] Continue beating until the buttercream is at room temperature and turns white. With the mixer running, add the cold butter, a few slices at a time, waiting for the butter to be incorporated before adding more. [3] When all the butter is fully incorporated, the buttercream is done. [4] The buttercream should be smooth with no sign of breaking or separating. If the buttercream appears to be separating, heat the bowl by nesting it in another bowl of hot water while stirring. When the buttercream comes back together, beat it again until cool.

Crème Fraîche

Nowadays most milk is pasteurized, a method of heating that kills harmful (and not so harmful) bacteria. When milk is left unpasteurized and the cream is skimmed off the top, that cream will gradually thicken. This is due to the bacteria it contains, which gradually multiply and convert lactose into lactic acid, giving crème fraîche its characteristic tang and causing it to thicken.

To make crème fraîche from pasteurized cream at home, we have to inoculate the cream with something that contains active bacteria, such as sour cream or buttermilk. When allowed to sit in a warm place, it ferments, causing the mixture to thicken up and develop its distinct tang.

The consistency of heavy cream before inoculation is about as thick as cultured buttermilk. [1] Add a small amount of sour cream—about ¼ cup/60 ml per 1 qt/1 L of cream. [2] Cover the cream with plastic wrap and leave it in a warm but not hot place (80°F/27°C) overnight. [3] As the cream first starts to thicken it will have the consistency of loose sour cream. You can use the cream at this point or continue to ferment it until it becomes very stiff. [4] Use stiff crème fraîche to make double cream (see page 202).

Double Cream

Most cream, including crème fraîche (see pages 200–201), contains about 37 percent butterfat. When crème fraîche gets very stiff, it's possible to drain it so that the excess water, or whey, it contains is eliminated and the percentage of butterfat reaches as high as 70 percent, creating double cream. The advantage of double cream is that it can be added to sauces as a thickener without subsequently having to reduce the sauce or the cream. Although double cream is readily available in the United Kingdom, it's difficult to get in North America, where many cooks want to make their own but are unsure of how to know when it's ready.

[1] Spoon stiff crème fraîche onto a clean sheet of fabric that has been thoroughly rinsed to eliminate residual fabric sizing or any soap. Pull together the corners of the cloth and tie it up into a bundle. [2] Drain the cream in a cool place for 24 hours. (I hang it from one of the racks in my refrigerator over a bowl to catch the runoff.)

Soft-Ball Sugar

When sugar and water are boiled together, the water gradually evaporates and creates a sugar syrup that thickens to various stages. Most anyone who has flipped through a baking book will have noticed the various degrees—threads, soft ball, hard ball, hard crack—for cooking sugar. Fortunately, there is rarely a need for sugar cooked to a stage other than soft ball.

Most books say to cook soft-ball sugar until a candy thermometer reaches 240°F/115°C. But what if you don't have a candy thermometer or if your thermometer isn't accurate? A better method is to dip a spoon into the hot syrup and then immediately dip the spoon in a glass of cold (but not iced) water and notice the sugar syrup's consistency. When the sugar syrup is still undercooked, it won't do much of anything when dipped in the water, but as it cooks and becomes more concentrated, the syrup will start to cling to the spoon and become pliable. When it takes on the consistency of chewed bubble gum after it has been dipped in the water, you've reached the soft-ball stage and should immediately remove the pan from the heat.

[1] Combine equal parts sugar and water in a heavy saucepan. **[2]** Put the sugar mixture over high heat and boil it until it reaches 240°F/115°C. **[3]** When the syrup coalesces into a firm yet malleable glob when dipped in cold water, the syrup is ready.

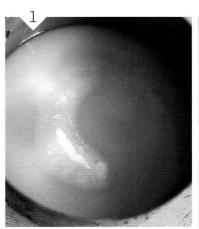

Caramel

True caramel is simply sugar that has been cooked until it melts and turns deep red. Caramel is used for making various desserts, including crème caramel, a custard that has been baked in a mold lined with caramel. It is also the base for caramel sauces and syrups.

Basic caramel shouldn't be confused with caramel syrup or caramel sauces. And butterscotch is something entirely different. If you add water to the still-hot caramel, the water will boil up and liquefy and turn the caramel into a syrup. If, instead, you add heavy cream, the cream will boil up, thicken, and create a caramel sauce that's perfect for ice cream. If you add butter to the hot caramel and then cream, you'll end up with butterscotch.

[1] You needn't follow the advice of some cooks and add water to the sugar before you cook it; you only need to put the sugar in a heavy-bottomed pan and cook it over medium heat while stirring. [2] You'll notice at first that lumps form. [3] Don't worry. These will gradually melt. If you keep stirring, all the lumps will have disappeared by the time the caramel is done. [4] Once the caramel turns deep red and starts to smoke, plunge the pan into a bowl of cold water (no need for ice) for a few seconds to stop the cooking.

Choux (Cream Puff Pastry)

To make cream puffs and profiteroles, you must first make choux batter, sometimes called *cream puff batter* or *cream puff pastry*. Whatever you call it, it is one of the easiest of all batters to make because it is cooked on the stove and doesn't need to be carefully rolled out.

[1] Melt butter in water over high heat. [2] When the water comes to a boil, add flour all at once. [3] Stir for about 1 minute, until the flour forms a single mass that holds together. Transfer the dough to a mixing bowl. [4] Work in eggs one by one and notice how the dough breaks up as you add each egg. [5] Stir the dough until it comes together before adding another egg. [6] You'll know you've added enough eggs when the dough passes two tests: First, it should form a rope when you lift a spoon out of it. [7] Second, when you use a spoon to make a deep groove in the batter, the groove should slowly close in on itself.

Place the puff pastry in a pastry bag and pipe the pastry onto an oiled baking sheet. (Or spoon the pastry onto the baking sheet.) Bake in a 425°F/220°C oven. [8] The puff pastry puffs as it bakes. [9] After the first 10 minutes of baking, continue baking the pastry in a low oven—about 300°F/150°C—to ensure the pastry is baked all the way through. When properly done, the puffed pastry should feel light when you toss one in your hand.

Brownies

Brownies are unique in that they are neither cake nor cookie. Some prefer brownies more cakelike; others want brownies that are more fudgelike. This introduces a variable when determining doneness—if the brownies are less cooked, they'll be fudgy (brownies); if cooked more thoroughly, they'll be cakey.

[1] To determine if the brownies are properly done, insert a knife in the center. If the knife comes out covered with wet, runny dough, the brownies are underdone and will be too wet to cut. If the knife comes out with some batter attached to it, the brownies will be fudgelike. [2] When the knife comes out clean, it indicates that the brownies are thoroughly done and cakelike. [3] Brownies that are baked until the knife comes out clean are easily cut into bars that hold their shape.

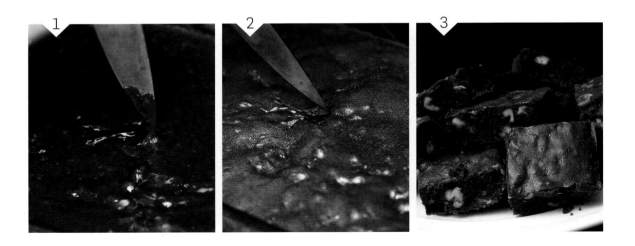

Cakes

A properly baked cake should bounce back to the touch when you press the surface gently with a finger. [1] If your finger leaves an imprint, it is most likely underdone. [2] Do the toothpick test to confirm: Insert a toothpick in the center of the cake. If it comes out with batter clinging to it, the cake is not yet done. [3] When the cake is done, the toothpick will come out clean.

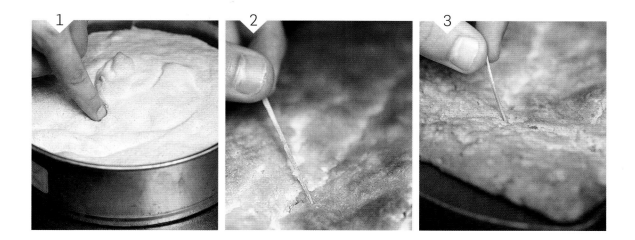

Berry Pie

Berry pies can be open-faced or covered with a top piecrust. The berries in a covered pie are usually combined with cornstarch to help the liquid they release thicken. I use a somewhat different method for covered pies and cook the berries for a few minutes at the beginning, just long enough to get them to release their liquid. Once the liquid has been released, I drain the berries and reduce the liquid in a sauté pan to concentrate its flavor. In this way, the berries are cooked for a minimum amount of time. When the amount of liquid has reduced by about half, add a small amount of cornstarch dissolved in water to thicken it. Typically, 1 teaspoon of cornstarch per 1 cup/240 ml of liquid is about right.

[1] To make a berry pie, combine berries with sugar and lime juice in a sauté pan deep enough to accommodate them and still be able to put a lid on top. Cover the pan and simmer the berries for about 10 minutes, just long enough for them to release their liquid. Strain the berries and set aside to cool, reserving the liquid. Return the liquid to the pan and simmer until it reduces by about half. [2] To thicken the liquid, whisk in a teaspoon of cornstarch that has been dissolved in a few teaspoons of water. Once the cooked berries and thickened liquid are ready, the pie can be assembled. [3] First, roll out a round of pie dough and place it in a pie plate. Spread the cooled berries on top of the dough. [4] Spoon the cooled liquid over the berries.

Roll the pastry dough lid over the pie filling, crimp the edges, and make slits in the dough. Bake the pie, about 1 hour in a 350°F/175°C oven, until the crust is brown and the liquid boils up through the slits. [5] If liquid isn't emerging from the slits, the best way to determine doneness is to insert a knife though a slit into the pie to see if it comes out clean, indicating the pie is done, or if it is covered in a still-liquidy filling, indicating it needs more time in the oven to set. [6] The finished berry pie will hold its shape when cooled to room temperature and sliced.

Bread Pudding

Bread pudding consists of cubes of bread baked in a custard mixture of eggs, milk, sugar, and vanilla. The amount of custard to add to a bread pudding is determined by the amount of bread. **[1]** The custard mixture should rise to the surface when you push on top of the unbaked bread pudding with a spatula, but should not cover the bread when it's just sitting there.

[2] When the pudding is finished cooking, you can determine doneness by pressing on it with the back of a spatula, at which point no liquid should rise to the surface. A paring knife inserted into the center should also come out clean.

Don't rely on the degree of browning as a measure of doneness, but rather control the browning with the oven temperature. If you notice the bread getting deep brown before the pudding has had a chance to set, lower the oven temperature. If, conversely, the pudding is setting up but the bread isn't browning, then the oven temperature should be increased.

A glass baking dish is best for bread pudding. Avoid using aluminum and cast-iron baking pans, which react with eggs and turn them gray. You will know you have overcooked your bread pudding if the custard breaks (separates) or curdles, or if the bread turns out soggy instead of fluffy.

Pancakes and Blinis

Pancakes are made much like crêpes except that crêpes contain no leavening. Pancakes are leavened with baking powder, a combination of chemicals that produce carbon dioxide gas when moistened. For this reason, pancake batter should be used within an hour of when it is made.

Blinis are a tasty pancake that is yeast-leavened and traditionally contains buckwheat flour. To cook them properly, you must determine not only the doneness of the pancakes themselves but also the doneness of the batter and of the yeast. Pancakes and blinis are cooked the same way.

[1] For blinis, combine active dry yeast with water, flour, and sugar. The yeast mixture should bubble up and rise after about 15 minutes (see Proofing Yeast page 216). Once you've confirmed that the yeast is viable, work the proofing mixture into your batter. Let the batter rise until it triples in volume before cooking it. Dollop the batter into a buttered nonstick frying pan over medium heat. For pancakes, ladle into the pan. **[2]** When bubbles form on the top and then pop, the blinis or pancakes are ready to be turned. **[3]** Cook them on the second side for about 3 minutes or until golden brown.

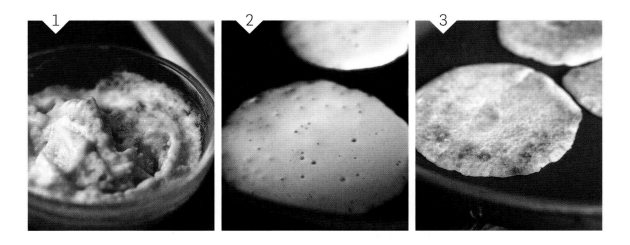

Popovers and Yorkshire Puddings

The only difference between a popover and Yorkshire pudding is that Yorkshire pudding is baked with the rendered fat from a beef roast. Both expand dramatically once baked into golden brown towers.

The trick to making popovers is to use the heaviest molds you can find. This is important because a heavy mold that's preheated will deliver heat immediately to the batter and cause it to rise. If you don't have heavy molds, try doubling up muffin tins or individual molds as shown here. Ideally, the molds should be made of metal since it delivers heat more quickly than ceramic or glass.

Preheat the molds in a 500°F/260°C oven. Brush with oil or, if you're making Yorkshire pudding, brush with the drippings from a roast, traditionally a beef rib roast, but any roast will do. Put the molds back in the oven and wait for the oven to come back to temperature. (You'll hear the oven turn on when you open the door. When the oven turns back off, you know it's at temperature again.) Working as quickly as you can, fill the molds about two-thirds of the way to the top with batter and immediately close the oven. [1] When the popovers double in height, after about 15 minutes, lower the oven temperature to 300°F/150°C so the popovers continue to cook through without falling or browning more. Cook for 5 minutes more.

1

Brioche

Brioche is essentially bread with a lot of butter and eggs in it. The yeast is proofed in the usual way (see "Proofing Yeast," page 216) and combined with flour and eggs. The mixture is worked in a mixer with the dough hook attachment and kneaded for about 7 minutes, until the dough pulls away from the sides of the mixer. One way of testing whether the dough is done is to touch it and see if it sticks. It should feel very sticky but not actually stick to your fingers.

Once you've made your basic dough with eggs and flour, it must be chilled slightly so it doesn't melt the butter. The cold butter is worked in a bit at a time, using a mixer with the paddle attachment, and the dough allowed to rise until tripled in volume. The dough is then punched down to deflate it and put in a loaf pan or fluted brioche mold, where it is allowed to rise until it comes up to the lip of the mold. It is then brushed with egg wash and baked in a 375°F/190°C oven.

There are three stages at which doneness is important: When the dough has been properly kneaded, properly proofed, and properly baked. Each of these stages has a signal that lets you know when you've completed it successfully.

Continued >>

[1] Combine eggs and flour in a mixer with the dough hook. Work proofed yeast into the dough. As you knead the dough you'll see it go through several stages. First, it's granular and then a liquid mass that sticks to the walls of the mixing bowl. [2] Then the dough will pull away from the sides of the mixing bowl.

[3] When the dough pulls away from the sides of the mixing bowl, add the cold butter a few slices at a time with the mixer on slow speed. [4] When the butter has all been added, the dough should again pull away from the sides of the mixing bowl. If the dough becomes too loose or runny, it's probably because the butter is too warm. Don't be tempted to add more flour. [5] Cover the dough with plastic wrap and let rise until tripled in volume.

[6] Punch down the dough to completely deflate it. Divide the dough into 8 equal pieces by using a pastry scraper to cut the dough in half and then cut each half into quarters. [7] Shape the portions into balls, and place the balls in a buttered nonstick loaf pan. Cover the loaf pan with plastic wrap. Let the dough rise until it comes close to the rim of the pan. [8] Brush the loaf with egg beaten with a teaspoon of water and a pinch of salt (egg wash). Bake the loaf until it sounds hollow when you thump on it with your finger. [9] The finished brioche will be golden brown and sound hollow when you tap the bottom.

Proofing Yeast

When using active dry yeast, it's a good idea to test it to make sure that it hasn't lost its strength. This test, called proofing, also activates the yeast so it acts more quickly once you work it into the dough.

To proof yeast, make a paste with a couple tablespoons each of flour and water, and a pinch of sugar. Add the yeast and let rise at room temperature for about 20 minutes. If the yeast doesn't bubble up or the flour mixture doesn't rise, the yeast is dead.

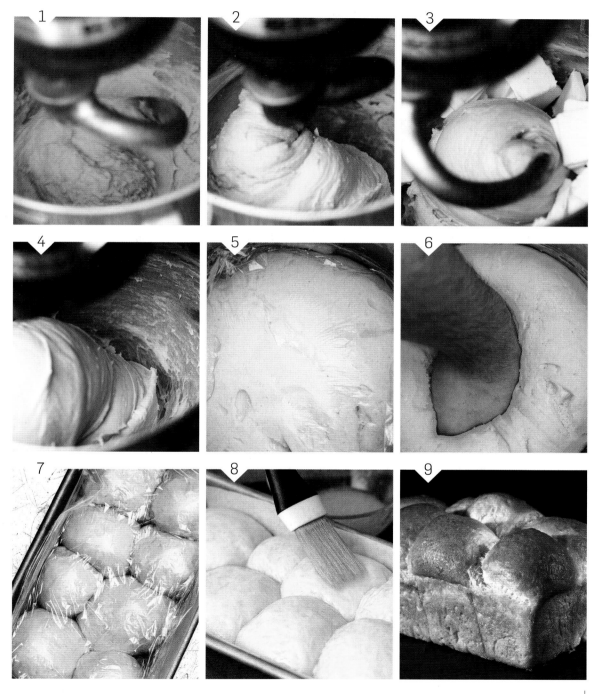

INDEX